Selecting, Buying, Installing and Using a Modern Warehouse Management System

By Jan Young

Selecting, Buying, Installing and Using a Modern Warehouse Management System

An Executive Briefing

By Jan Young
EB-004

Copyright © 2006, 2009 by Jan B Young
All Rights Reserved

Cover photo by author

ISBN 978-0-557-05915-7

Table of Contents

Introduction 1
   Purpose of this Paper 1
   About the Author 2
Warehouse Management Systems 3
   Purpose 3
   Core Function 4
   Core Data 8
   Basic Processes and Functions 10
   Additional Processes and Functions 18
   Industry-Specific Function and Feature 33
   Features and Functions Not Included 37
WMS Costs and Benefits 39
   ERP Systems vs. Best-of-Breed 40
   Hardware and Infrastructure Costs 40
   Software Costs 46
   Other Project Costs 47
   Ongoing Operating Costs 55
   Benefits 59
   Calculating ROI 69
   WMS Weaknesses 69
   Organizational Impact 70
   Who Should Have a WMS? 73
The WMS Project 74
   First Time vs. Reinstallation 74
   Make vs. Buy 75
   Timeline Expectations 76
   Achieving Success 77
   Project Staff Turnover 79
   User-Supplier Relations 80
Commercially Available Systems 83
   Brief Industry History 83
   Major Product Options 84
   Dealing in the Market Today 86
Buying a WMS 90
   Identify Concept 91

- Form Project Team 92
- Identify Needs 94
- Contact Suppliers and Select Initial Group 101
- Create and Issue RFI 102
- Select Short List 104
- Create and Issue RFQ 105
- Final Supplier Selection 109
- Contract Negotiation 112

The Installation Project 113
- Before Installing 114
- Kickoff Meeting 114
- Conference Room Pilot 116
- Modification and Preparation 118
- Installation 119
- Mock Go-Live 120
- Final Review 122
- Go-Live 123

Ongoing Operation 124
- Monitoring 124
- Maintaining 125
- Extending Value 126
- Upgrades 127
- Maintaining Supplier Relations 128

Summary 131
Appendix A – Entity Relationship Diagrams 132
Appendix B – ROI Calculation Worksheet 133
Appendix C – Reference Questions 139

Introduction

Purpose of this Paper

The purchase of a warehouse management system (WMS) is like the purchase of your first house. It is a major financial transaction, representing a major commitment to the future, but with only imperfect knowledge of what you're buying and what the consequences will be. While the concepts behind warehouse management systems have been proven through thousands of successful installations all over the world, it is also a fact that a significant proportion of those installations were only successful on the second or even the third costly attempt.

This executive briefing is written for the executive who is considering the installation of a warehouse management system in a currently un-automated supply chain. It contains, however, a significant amount of information of value to those who have been through the process and are now in maintenance and operation mode. It may also have special value to those who are dissatisfied with their present system and are considering a replacement.

The remarks included in this briefing apply equally well whether you outsource all or part your supply chain, or whether you perform all functions internally. Unless you have contracted with a 3PL for use of its warehouse management system, the issues faced, the processes required, and the costs and benefits are identical. There are, of course, benefits to the 3PL of having a single system for all of its customers, but there are also benefits within a company of having a single system for all of its 3PLs.

We begin with the purpose of warehouse management systems and a description of their costs and benefits. The build-versus-buy choice is discussed. Organizational impact and the short and long-term effect on your customers are described. The briefing then moves into a detailed description of how to buy a WMS. This description covers the project team that must be assembled, the marketplace for commercial systems, the types of systems available and how you should go about choosing among them, the creation of a Request for Proposal and the evaluation of RFP responses. It also provides a methodology for justifying/funding a warehouse management system and concludes with discussions of system installation and maintenance.

About the Author

Jan Young is a trained Industrial Engineer with thirty-eight years experience in manufacturing and distribution. He has:

- Managed a factory and a warehouse employing over a hundred workers in a 24/7/365 continuous operation

- Sold, installed, configured and maintained both manufacturing planning and warehouse management systems on a global scale for more than thirty years

- Designed a warehouse management system. That system, aimed at the top-tier market, is now one of the premier, commercially-available systems

- Operated a private consulting and publishing business for fifteen years

- Consulted in more than fifty warehouses in ten countries on three continents

Now retired, Mr. Young has freed himself from all commercial attachments and is in a position to provide unbiased consul. While he is no longer accepting new consulting clients, he will respond to serious questions about this book sent to *j.b.young@presys.biz*.

Warehouse Management Systems

In this section we define the term "warehouse management system" and, in following sections, describe the costs and benefits of such systems and set them in the context of other supply chain systems.

The discussions below outline:

1. The purpose of a warehouse management system
2. Core warehouse management system functions
3. Data required to support core functions
4. The basic processes provided in a warehouse management system and key features associated with these processes
5. Additional processes and features provided in almost all warehouse management systems
6. Industry-specific processes and features provided in many warehouse management systems

Purpose

The purpose of a warehouse management system is to automate and refine the management of the inventory in a warehouse, warehouse space, the people who work in the warehouse and the time available to accomplish warehouse tasks. In an appropriate environment with good technical and operational management, this automation can significantly increase productivity, improve customer service, and enhance asset utilization. Warehouse management systems have been known to pay for themselves in as little as six months, but paybacks of one to two years are more common.

A warehouse management system provides controls at an appropriate level so that business rules can be encoded into the system and, to a significant degree, the system can run itself with only oversight on the part of supervisors and engineers.

It also provides data and analytical tools so management can critique the business rules on an ongoing basis allowing optimization of operations. The net result is that senior management is freed from many day-to-day operational considerations and can therefore concentrate on larger issues with greater long-term value.

Core Function

We begin with a definition of what a warehouse management system is and what it does. While most users of warehouse management systems understand very well what they do, few have an understanding of the theoretical underpinnings, and thus few have an understanding of the potentials (and potential weaknesses) of these systems. This description, of course, deals only with modern, full-function warehouse management systems. Many older and less-robust systems will do only some of the processes described.

Modern full-function warehouse management systems include seven core functions, each of which consists of many processes and features. The core functions are:

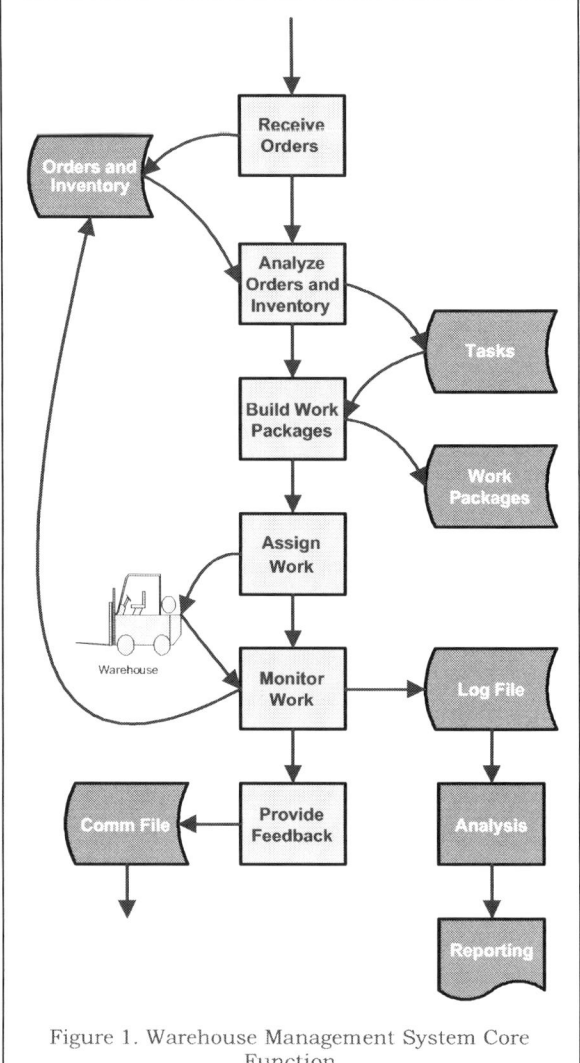

Figure 1. Warehouse Management System Core Function

1. <u>Receive orders.</u> The direct entry of inbound and outbound orders[1] into a warehouse management system is rare; the great majority of systems include a process that receives and preprocesses both inbound and outbound orders from other systems. Orders are subsequently used as the basis for almost all warehouse work.

2. <u>Define work.</u> A second core process uses orders and inventory data to determine work that must be done in the warehouse. The basic principle is

---

[1] Inbound orders include purchase orders, requisitions, work orders, and incoming transfer orders from other warehouses or plants. Outbound orders include all forms of shipment orders including sales orders, customer orders and outgoing transfer orders.

that no work should be done unless it contributes to the completion of an order, either directly or indirectly. Warehouse management systems, therefore, begin with orders and determine the picking, packing, shipping, receiving and putaway work needed, together with the pick location replenishments that are required as a consequence of picking. This planning process usually runs in background and results in lists of tasks that are stored pending further processing.

Different systems name the work definition process differently. In some instances it is called "wave building" because it runs in batch mode, produces batches of work, and those batches constitute a pick wave. In other instances it may be called "allocation" because it necessarily allocates inventory as part of the planning process. Regardless of the name, however, all full function warehouse management systems plan work at the level of the individual material movement, specifying at least:

1. The item or SKU
2. The quantity
3. The type of work to be done
4. The specific location in the warehouse where the work is to begin
5. The specific location where the work is to end

3. <u>Organize work.</u> Because warehouses are typically large and involve significant worker travel, the organization of work is important. The third warehouse management system core process is the development of work packages, ready for assignment to operators as they become available. These work packages typically are designed to maximize productivity and are usually organized considering:

1. Type of work (receiving, picking, replenishing, etc.)
2. Vehicle/equipment requirements
3. Zone or other geographic location in the warehouse
4. Priority or importance of the work
5. Some limitation on the size of a work package

Once defined, the work packages are sorted into a logical and efficient operating sequence, usually driven by a combination of warehouse travel distance and an efficient operating pattern. Some warehouse management systems build work packages in a batch process that automatically follows work definition; others build and organize the packages dynamically as part of the following dispatching process.

4. <u>Dispatch work.</u> As workers become available (either having just arrived in the warehouse or having just completed another assignment), a real-time process examines the work available, the operator's skills, the equipment (lift trucks) in use and the operator's current location. With this

information in hand, it dynamically assigns another package of work to the operator, usually choosing the highest priority work available.

5. <u>Control and monitor work.</u> With work assigned to an operator, most warehouse systems direct the work in step-by-step detail using one or more real-time processes and some form of portable computing that moves with the operator. This process not only directs the operator through the work to assure efficiency and accuracy, but also collects validating information and uses it to update its tables and to generate updating transactions for other systems. Updates usually made by the control and monitoring processes include order status and inventory levels in individual warehouse locations.

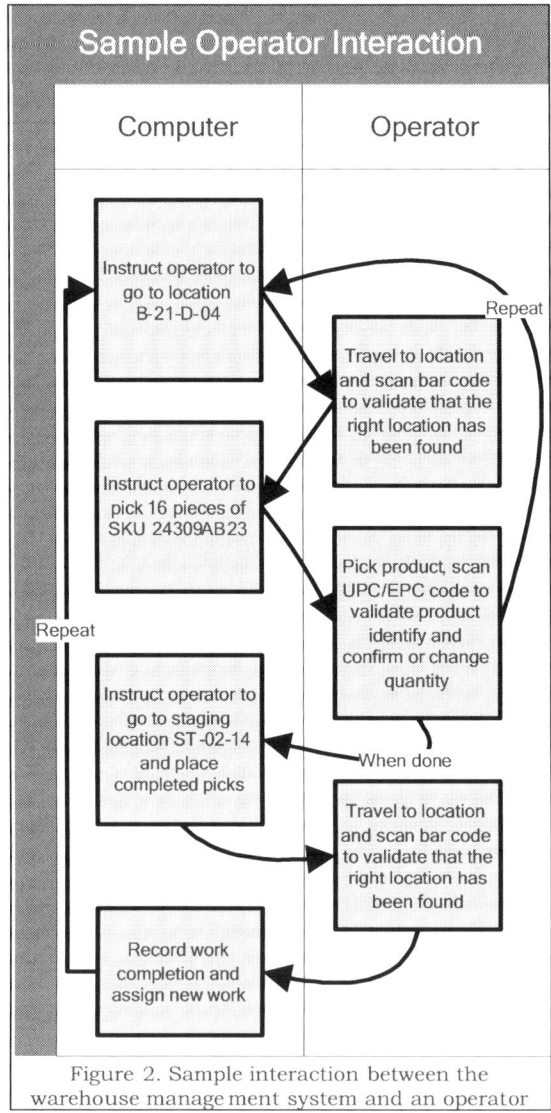

Figure 2. Sample interaction between the warehouse management system and an operator

The validation of work as it is performed is accompanied by operator feedback mechanisms that come into play when errors are made or when exceptions are found. The operator is, for instance, given immediate real-time feedback if the location scanned does not match the system's expectation, or if the wrong SKU or item is handled. Similarly, if the pick quantity does not match the quantity planned, validation can take any of a wide variety of actions, depending on the availability of inventory elsewhere, management's control settings, and other factors. These exception-handling processes are not shown in the diagram in Figure 2.

On completion of a package of work, control is passed back to the dispatch function for assignment of the next work package to the operator.

6. <u>Provide host feedback.</u> As work is completed, the warehouse management system provides feedback to the various "host" systems, allowing them to maintain their databases in parallel. This feedback is typically used by the host systems to do many things, most always including:

   1. Triggering of invoicing for customer shipments
   2. Authorization of invoice payment for supplier receipts
   3. Updating of inventory records and the balance sheet
   4. Building of payroll data

7. <u>Maintain an audit trail.</u> As work is completed and validated, most good warehouse management systems maintain a detailed audit trail at the level of the individual material movement. The resulting log file can, over time, be very large, but because it contains detailed and validated information, it can be a very important source of management analysis and information. Some warehouse management systems provide analytical and reporting tools internally, while others rely on third-party tools. In either case, the availability of this data is often poorly understood and the data itself is often underutilized.

These seven core functions are the basis of any good warehouse management system. Systems that do not include these core functions are generally not classified as "warehouse management" systems. Additional functions (discussed starting on page 18) are often included.

The ability to scan and print bar codes is not described here as warehouse management system function because it is provided almost entirely by hardware: scanners and printers. All reasonable warehouse management systems, however, include bar code capability.

Core Data

Necessary to the core processes, warehouse management systems maintain complex databases of linked tables containing data files on a wide variety of subjects. Accuracy of this data is paramount because with inaccurate data, system results are necessarily inaccurate and objectives cannot be reached.

The most important data maintained by warehouse management systems includes orders, items, locations and inventories. These data entities are related as shown in the diagram at the right. See Appendix A (page 132) for a brief explanation of the notation in the diagram.

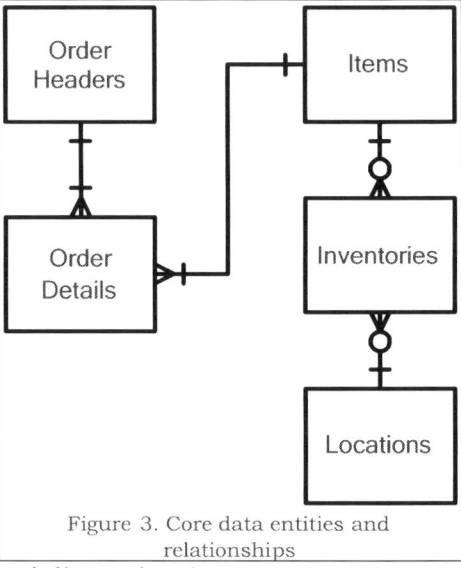

Figure 3. Core data entities and relationships

- Item data. The item master table is generally extensive, containing one or more item identifiers (item numbers), descriptions, various classifications, dimensional data, packaging data and much more. Many warehouse management system item master tables carry data that is found nowhere else in the business (such as product weights and dimensions).

- Locations. Although terminology may vary from system to system, a location is generally a geographic subdivision of the warehouse in which inventory may be stored, either temporarily or for the long term. Locations are often configured to be single pallet positions, floor storage lanes, or bins, but most warehouse management systems allow a great deal of flexibility in their configuration.

  The most powerful and flexible warehouse management systems define a "location" as a place where multiple items or SKUs can be stored if necessary, but is small enough so that the system does not attempt to track the physical placement of product within the location, assuming that the operator can find things easily by visual inspection.

- Inventories. In a warehouse management system, inventory records are maintained at the item and location level. That is, an individual record tells the system the on-hand quantity of a specific item in a specific location. Most systems also provide for separate inventories for different manufacturing lots of an item and allow for other inventory characteristics such as a product grade (firsts, seconds, etc.), quality status (on hold pending disposition, released, etc.), product availability, and other information.

- Orders. Warehouse management systems also maintain data on both inbound and outbound orders. Order data maintained on the warehouse management system can be extensive, particularly on the outbound side. Some systems maintain data on blanket orders, others only on individual releases.

Additional tables supplement the core:

- Operators or warehouse workers. Some systems maintain extensive data about skills and training levels for use in work assignment.

- Material handling vehicles. When an operator is paired with a vehicle, the result is a capability profile. The term "vehicle" should be understood broadly. Un-powered carts and even "afoot" are acceptable vehicles.

- Inventory storage devices. All inventories are stored in storage devices, which specify the capabilities of a location. Like "vehicle," "storage device" is a broad term including open floor storage and even outside or yard storage.

- Customers. Customer data maintained at the warehouse system level is usually limited to the information needed to make delivery. Name and address, for instance, would be included, but credit rating usually would not be.

- Suppliers. Like customers, supplier data maintained in the warehouse management system is usually limited.

- Carriers. Depending on the warehouse management system's transportation capabilities, extensive carrier data may be maintained or, in some systems, this data is relegated to an attached transportation management system (TMS)

And these tables are supplemented by dozens (possibly hundreds) of additional tables containing lists of pending work, records of completed work and a wide variety of control information. Most tables at this level are internal, being maintained entirely by the system but are sometimes quite useful for reporting and analysis.

Essentially all warehouse management systems include interfaces with external systems so that information in the large data tables can be shared.

Generally the warehouse management system is considered a user of master data and primary maintenance responsibility is assigned elsewhere, but there are two major exceptions: the location and inventory tables. The warehouse management system is usually considered to maintain the master location table because the information on this table often appears nowhere else in the business. It maintains the master inventory table because it maintains inventory records in more detail than do other systems. The distinction between the master and slave copies of the data is important to the design and construction of the interfaces. This is particularly important with relation to the item table, which is often a blend of host-maintained and warehouse-maintained data.

Basic Processes and Functions

Beyond the core processes, modern warehouse management systems are usually delivered with a broad variety of process features and functions aimed at optimizing both system efficiency and warehouse performance. Some of the most important are:

➢ Warehouse Structure. The warehouse management system allows management to define and maintain the physical and logical organization of the warehouse in control tables. This structure is used within the system to assist in the organization and execution of work.

- o Warehouse zones and sub-zones are defined as groups of locations. Some zones or sub-zones may have dynamic definitions. Others are fixed.
- o Warehouse aisles are defined as a different grouping of locations
- o Pick paths are defined as a location sequence or, sometimes, the need to define a sequence may be eliminated by specifying that picks will be done in location number sequence. Most warehouse management systems also allow for dynamic pick path development to support s-pattern travel[2]. Many support intra-aisle x-patterns and z-patterns and specialized pick patterns for side loaders, cranes and other equipment.
- o Individual location dimensions, location positions relative to each other and to the total warehouse, and location elevations above the floor are

---

[2] S-pattern travel involves traveling adjacent aisles in the opposite direction and is dynamic when a skipped aisle can cause subsequent aisle sequences to reverse.

all important to the development of work plans, as is identification of the type of equipment in use.
- Storage devices (pallet racking, carton flow rack, floor storage, etc.) are defined for each location. These device definitions support process variations as needed to optimize processes and movement in the warehouse.
- Locations can optionally be dedicated to a single item, or can be left undedicated, which allows the warehouse management system to use them for different items at different times as necessary.
- The storage of multiple items in a single location is supported, but not necessarily encouraged.

- <u>Work Definition.</u> The basic processes that develop the lists of work needed in the warehouse often have several important features:

  - Orders received from an external system can be immediately planned, or can be held and released into the planning process through a number of mechanisms. These releasing mechanisms can be aimed at prioritization of the work, timing of it to meet customer needs, or coordination of certain work attributes in the warehouse. For example, waves of work can be built for a certain type of product, or for a chosen carrier, or for almost any order attribute or combination or attributes
  - Order releasing mechanisms in most warehouse management systems provide for limits to the size of a wave. These limits may be specified in terms of a quantity of orders, a quantity of lines, a limiting labor requirement (standard hours), or a similar measure.
  - Most warehouse management systems allow orders to be released into the work definition process automatically according to predefined logic, or manually at a user's request
  - The order planning process generally combines multiple orders for a single customer into a single entity for efficient picking and shipping, while retaining separate records for each of the orders to accommodate host systems and invoicing. These order consolidation capabilities usually support exemption flags at both the order and customer levels.
  - Most warehouse management systems allow wave-building queries to be saved as templates for future use and also allow planners to specify that the resulting work should either be immediately released for execution on the warehouse floor, or should be held for review before release.
  - Management and supervision is given an opportunity to view labor requirements by zone, by vehicle type, by work class and in other ways. The view is generally enabled for work that has not yet been planned (useful for a longer term look ahead), for work that has been planned, but not yet released, and for work in progress.

- Some warehouse management systems allow management to cancel waves or parts of a wave, withdraw the planned work from the work queues, and return orders to their original, unplanned status. This process, however, can be extremely complicated when a portion of the work has already been completed, so automatic facilities within the warehouse management system are often limited.
- Order planning processes allocate (or reserve) product during the planning processes to prevent duplication
- Many warehouse management systems deal with multiple units of measure, allowing the customer, for instance, to order in dozens, while the product is inventoried in cases of sixty and is priced per hundred.
- The work definition processes include user-definable rules or controls that determine where and how the components of an order will be picked. These controls normally consider such things as the customer, the type of order, the age of the material in various locations in the warehouse, the quantity ordered by the customer, the handling unit needed (pallet, carton, or each), and other factors. Many systems provide tools for the validation of these complex rules.
- To facilitate the building of pick waves by carrier and to support shipment consolidation (and for other reasons), most warehouse management systems support an optional interface with a transportation management system[3] that allows carrier selection to occur either immediately following receipt of the order from the host, or just prior to its inclusion in a wave.

➢ Receiving. The basic receiving process involves identifying and counting receipts, reconciling them against a purchase order or inbound transfer order, and then launching a following process to determine where the arriving product should be stored, reserve space for it, and create a putaway task. Important receiving features included in most warehouse management systems are:

- Receiving can be done either through a mobile/RF device or using a desktop system client
- Receiving can be "blind," or not[4]
- Product can be received against an order or without reference to an order

---

[3] For purposes of this paper, transportation management systems are considered separate from warehouse management systems, although some could disagree with the definition.

[4] "Blind" receiving implies that the receiver does not know in advance what items or quantities are to be received. By forcing the receiver to identify and count product, accuracy is improved, but at the cost of additional effort on the part of the receivers. Different companies prefer different methods.

- Receiving processes can apply to returns as well as the arrival of new goods from suppliers
- Over and under receipt tolerances are supported and receivers are warned if these tolerances are violated
- Receipts can be made against inbound orders (purchase orders, transfer orders, etc.), ASNs (advanced shipment notices), both, or neither (without order).
- Advanced Shipment Notices (ASNs) can be received at any level from the single piece to the container load. ASN receiving can consist of no more than a single bar code scan, or can involve teardown and detailed inspection and counting of the load, depending on management's wishes and experience with the supplier.
- Receiving processes allow for the receipt of mixed SKUs on a pallet
- Damage can be identified and recorded during the receiving process
- The receiving process handles notes and special instructions at the order, item, and supplier levels
- The receiving process handles multiple units of measure and multiple packaging levels (carton, pallet, etc) and allows the receiving operator to work at the most convenient level using the most convenient unit of measure
- Product attributes can be captured (with system-provided defaults) during the receiving process. Attributes that can be captured include lot number, serial number, country of origin, material grade, product ownership and more.
- Receiving processes will accept preprinted license plate numbers or generate them as needed.
- A receiving document can be printed following receipt
- Receiving supports optional QA/Inspection processes that result in either pass-fail or in product grading[5].
- Receiving processes include a set of rules that can be used to define when a supervisor needs to review and approve a receipt before it occurs.

> Putaway. Once product has been received into the warehouse, the next step is to find a place to put it and then get it put away. Many people consider this process, together with the receiving process, to be the most important in the warehouse because, if product is received and stored properly, records will be accurate and the outbound processes will have at least a chance of efficiency. Incorrect receiving or putaway, however, dooms the rest of the warehouse to a constant inefficient search for material.

---

[5] Few warehouse management systems (if any) support true quality inspection processes. If the simplified processes supported by the warehouse management system are insufficient in a specific business, it may be necessary to interface the warehouse management system with a separate quality management system.

- The selection of locations can be driven by user-defined rules which consider product quality, velocity, the size and other physical characteristics of the product and the storage locations, the quantity and packaging level of the receipt, the existence of dedicated storage locations (if any), product hazards, the distribution of product already in the warehouse, and the age of the product received relative to product already in the warehouse.
- Locations can be selected for each of the SKUs on a multi-SKU pallet or for the pallet as a whole.
- Location selection routines can direct product to forward picking instead of reserve, thereby eliminating the effort and cost of a replenishment move.
- A tool is provided for validation of the location selection rules.
- The putaway process is system-directed. The system determines where the product will be stored and directs the operator to that location.
- The putaway process allows operators to override system-selected locations and validates proper placement of the material
- The putaway operator can put away a single receipt, a mixed-SKU pallet, or groups of receipts. When the operator puts away product to more than one storage location, the system provides an efficient route through the warehouse.

➢ Replenishment. Warehouse management systems automatically determine when the replenishment of forward picking location is needed and manage the work.

- The need for replenishment is usually driven by a threshold or trigger point, but other methods are also supported in some systems
- The quantity to be replenished is also system determined, often based on the available capacity of the forward pick location together with the availability and physical location of reserve stocks
- The source of replenishment material is determined by rules similar to, but separate from the rules that determine where orders are picked. These rules consider units of measure (cases, pallets or eaches) as necessary.
- Replenishment rules support multiple forward pick locations for a single product
- Replenishment on an off-shift daily cycle is supported along with replenishment done in-line while pick work is active
- Replenishment execution is RF directed in real time with user-configurable priorities

- Picking. In most warehouses, picking is the single largest labor classification and thus the most costly activity. As a result, it has the greatest potential for cost reduction and receives the most attention. Warehouse management systems thus generally support a broad array of methods and options.

    Basic picking methods supported by warehouse management systems include the following. Essentially all of these methods are available for application within a single warehouse zone (called zone picking) or across the entire warehouse (called unzoned picking). Essentially all are applied to the picks demanded by a single wave, as defined in the work definition process described above.

    - Order picking. The picker is responsible for all of the items required for a single order.
    - Shipment picking. The picker picks all products required for a shipment. Shipment picking can include multiple orders from the same customer if they are to be shipped together, or, in the extreme, may include all orders from multiple customers that will comprise a single shipment.
    - Cluster picking. The picker is responsible for making all picks required in a dynamically determined small area of the warehouse. The content of a cluster is usually determined anew for each pick wave and usually contains multiple orders from multiple customers intended to leave the warehouse in multiple shipments.
    - Batch picking. The picker is responsible for picking everything needed for a group of orders (a batch) in a predefined area in the warehouse.
    - Carrier picking. The picker is responsible for picking everything needed for a single, specific carrier. This method is often available for a single carrier trailer and can enforce multi-stop load sequencing and fluid loading when necessary.
    - Pick and pass, also known as progressive picking. In this method, pickers are dedicated to zones or sub-zones. Each picker picks everything required in his or her zone, places the picks into a carton or tote for each order, and passes the completed work on to another picker in another zone. When the last zone is completed, the orders are then complete without the need for an accumulation step.
    - The "bucket brigade." A bucket brigade is a variation on the pick-and-pass theme in which the dividing lines between zones or pickers are dynamically determined based on individual picker speeds.
    - Full pallet picking. Separate processes are almost always provided for full pallet picking because (a) the equipment requirements are different and (b) the process requires optimization differently since pickers will make a separate trip into the warehouse for each pallet (or two pallets).

Most warehouse management systems include size limits that allow large pick tours to be divided among several pickers when the limits are exceeded, despite the fact that we have described them here the work done by "the picker."

These basic pick methods generally include a variety of optional features, selectable by management based on item and order requirements and, in some cases, on other considerations.

- Live loading. When picks (or groups of picks) are complete, the picker can be directed to load them immediately on the outbound trailer. Live loading works best in a full-pallet environment and for single-stop loads, but can be managed for multi-stop loads when a single operator can be assigned to pick the entire trailer. Live loading is also sometimes called direct or fluid loading.
- Material validation. Pickers can be required to confirm that they are picking the correct material from the correct location, usually by scanning bar codes or reading RFID tags on the locations and/or products.
- Delivery validation. Pickers can be required to confirm that completed picks have been loaded or staged correctly, again by scanning bar codes or reading RFID tags.
- Other validations. Pickers can also be required to capture or confirm serial numbers and/or lot numbers as picking progresses. Some systems also can be configured to require operators to make other validations (such as material grade, color, etc.)
- Cartonization, also known as carton selection. Warehouse management systems often can use sophisticated routines to pre-select the size of carton or tote required for an order, eliminating the need for a picker to guess. This ability can significantly reduce the cube shipped and can eliminate much repacking.
- RF or paper. Many warehouse management systems provide the ability to direct pickers either through a printed pick list or, in real time, using RF terminals.
- Pick labels. Many warehouse management systems can print pick labels for application to the product or to the pick containers. These labels can serve many purposes including carrier or customer compliance, price ticketing, etc. They can also replace printed pick lists and RF terminals.
- Vehicle and equipment sensitivity. Pick methods also need to vary depending on the equipment in use. Piece picks made in a single aisle, for example, need to be presented to the picker in a different sequence for side-loader lift trucks than for conventional equipment.

- Order assembly, packing, staging and shipping. These processes may be combined into a single post-picking process in some systems, or may be separate.

    o Order assembly. When several pickers pick an order, its components must be brought together for palletization and/or packing plus shipment.
    o Packing. Physical packing of the product for shipment is required, but only for certain items in specified quantities and then only if they have not been picked directly into a shippable container.
    o Staging. All completed orders must be staged pending loading (unless live loading is in use). Load assembly is accomplished as part of the staging operation.
    o Loading. The warehouse management system directs the loading of outbound trailers using RF terminals and bar codes on docks/doors or the trailers themselves to verify that the loading is done correctly. RF is also used to close trailers and indicate completion so the yard management system can direct their movement and placement of the next one.
    o Shipping. Shipping processes in a warehouse management system generally include management of the loading of a trailer and preparation of bills of lading, master bills and/or a freight manifest. The best warehouse management systems are capable of sharing this workload appropriately with a transportation management system or a parcel manifesting system if one is in use.

Most warehouse management systems support the following features and options in the post-picking arena:

o Intelligent routing. Not all picks go through all processes. Full pallets, for instance, need not be packed; live loads need not be staged; orders picked entirely by a single person need not be accumulated, etc.
o Labeling. The warehouse management system prints labels (address labels, carrier compliance labels, customer-specific compliance labels, etc.) and packing lists as needed.
o Pallet flexibility. Pallets can be reconfigured on the dock.
o Direction and validation. The warehouse management system determines the movement of material needed through the various warehouse processes. It directs that movement using RF terminals and validates that the work is done correctly through either bar code or RFID scans. Validation can also include confirmation that the load is properly configured and is complete, and that it is loaded on the right trailer.
o Packing and checking instructions. The warehouse management system provides packing instructions according to management rules

and customer and carrier specification. It also can lead the packer (or a separate checker) through an order checking process.
- Interfaces. Warehouse management systems interface seamlessly and in real time with transportation management, parcel manifesting, and yard management systems[6].
- Communication technologies. Warehouse management systems include the ability to communicate with customers, suppliers and carriers (external business entities) via either EDI or XML (over the Internet). Third-party tools are sometimes used.

Additional Processes and Functions

Few significant warehouse management systems provide only the processes listed above. The labeling of the processes described below as "additional" should not be taken to mean they are unimportant. Some are critical to the successful operation of a warehouse management system.

➢ Material handling equipment interfaces. These interfaces allow the warehouse management system to work directly with automated equipment, primarily carousels, AS/RS equipment, and sortation systems. Although many software suppliers claim "standard" off-the-shelf interfaces, their implementation almost always involves some degree of customization. The standard interfaces, where they exist, however, do serve to reduce the amount and cost of the customization required.

➢ Other interfaces. In addition to interfaces mentioned above, warehouse management systems almost always provide interfaces to:

- Business systems. The interfaces to the user's business systems (such as an ERP system) are used for order downloading and for uploading of shipments, receipts and inventory adjustments. The best warehouse management systems are capable of interfacing with multiple business systems, even including instances of shared host responsibility[7]).

---

[6] This paper considers transportation management and parcel manifesting to be external to the warehouse management system. Yard management is considered an internal function of warehouse management systems, but is discussed later. Some systems support different definitions.

[7] Shared host responsibility includes instances in which, for instance, separate plants produce the same product using different business systems, where orders for a single customer may be sent to the warehouse management system from different sources, etc.

- Slotting systems. The slotting interface is used to download status and activity to the slotting system and to upload planned product location changes and movements[8].
- Transportation management systems. TMS interfaces generally operate (1) when orders are downloaded, (2) when orders are planned, and/or (3) when picking and packing is complete. The term "transportation management system" includes carrier selection systems, parcel manifesting systems, fleet management and truck routing systems, and more.

➤ <u>Multiple warehouse management.</u> High-end warehouse management systems are capable of supporting a network of company warehouses, rather than just a single facility. This capability has several components.

- Technically, multiple facilities can be managed either by multiple instances of the warehouse management system installed on a single server, or within a single database. This capability sometimes makes it possible to justify a warehouse management system installation in a network of very small warehouses where hardware costs would otherwise be prohibitive. The downside, however, is that a system failure or capacity limitation affects multiple facilities, generally reducing reliability.
- Possibly more significant, the concept of multiple warehouse management includes the ability to better manage transfer shipments between facilities. If, for instance, a transfer order is entered in one location (or by a host computer), the warehouse management system will represent it as a shipment for one warehouse and as a receipt for the other. Depending on company policies, the receiving warehouse might even be relieved of the need to inspect and count the material and might only need to put it away.
- Multiple warehouse management also includes the ability to cross-dock shipments from one warehouse to a remote customer through another warehouse. In the right circumstances, this can save significant transportation expense. (Cross docking is considered in more detail later in this briefing.)
- And, at the very highest end, the network of warehouse management systems can accept customer orders from a host system and internally decide which warehouse(s) should ship the material. Such decisions would be made based on distance (transportation cost) from the customer, on available inventory, and possibly on the backlog of work in the individual warehouses. These systems can even automatically define and execute inter-warehouse transfer orders based on a

---

[8] Some warehouse management systems include slotting function as an internal component. This paper considers them to be separate systems, outside of the scope of discussion.

management-defined set of rules. The ultimate function approaches that of a distribution requirements system (and can even incorporate one).

- Value added services (VAS). The addition of manufacturing or quasi-manufacturing functions to the warehouse is a relatively recent phenomenon, but is becoming more common as many markets tend toward product customization, on-demand configuration and the principles of postponement. Examples of value-added services include monogramming (apparel), packing in custom boxes (automotive and parts), gift wrap (retail), assembly, software installation and configuration (computers and electronics), and kitting (many industries).

  Support provided for value-added services in most warehouse management systems relates in many respects to the support provided by manufacturing shop floor systems. Specific features usually provided include:

    o The warehouse management system defines the need for value-added work based, usually, on management rules and open or forecast orders, but also optionally on production orders produced by another system. It determines the material movements required, directs material handlers via RF as the moves are made, obtains validation that the moves are made correctly, and directs movement to succeeding workstation, to packing/shipping, or back to stock as needed.
    o Value added services are supported either inbound, (after product receipt but before putaway, outbound (after picking), or for stock (between putaway and picking).
    o The WMS monitors the usage of floor stock items and plans and directs their replenishment. Backflushing[9] is normally used for inventory control at the workstations themselves.
    o It supports the bills of material necessary to determine the items required to do assembly
    o It supports disassembly operations often associated with returns handling
    o It supports inspection operations and the associated condition codes
    o The warehouse management system provides production reporting
    o It supports the assignment of lot numbers and/or serial numbers to completed product

- Returns processing and reverse logistics. Nearly all warehouses receive returns from customers and the handling of these returns can be a major headache. In addition, some businesses ship product in totes or other

---

[9] Backflushing is a technique whereby the completion of a group of assemblies causes the system to automatically relive workstation inventories based on a bill of material.

returnable or recyclable packaging and sometimes these containers must be tracked to assure that they do, in fact, come back.

A complete returns processing and reverse logistics function can be complex, involving a significant number of sub-functions.

- Authorization and Planning. The authorization and planning function is accessible either to end customers (usually over the Internet), or locally, or both, depending on configuration. It identifies users and determines their authority to make returns, and collects information about the material to be returned. It analyzes the user's request, product warranties and other information to determine approval, determines whether or not a replacement shipment is required, determines whether or not a service call is required and communicates approval and terms. Finally, it receives acceptance from the user, determines material disposition[10], plans transportation, prints shipping labels/documents, prepares an ASN for the destination, and issues of credit memos and deposit refunds where physical product receipt and inspection is not required.
- Receiving. The detailed receiving function is similar to the standard warehouse management system receiving function. Receipts may be made against ASNs, against orders, or without reference to either an ASN or an order. When a receipt is made against an ASN and when UCC128 labels are provided for each handling unit, detailed counting may be required or omitted, based on rules established by the user.

    Some arriving handling units are contained within returnable containers and some consist entirely of empty returnable containers. As returnable containers arrive, they are identified and counted or, if serialized, individually scanned. The returnables repository (below) is notified of the arrival.

    Under some circumstances, arrival of an item is sufficient to trigger credit to the returning customer or payment to the shipping vendor. In other circumstances, inspection is required. Generally the rules to determine credit/payment requirements are established by vendor, customer, carrier, order, item and/or item status.

    Some arriving items not requiring inspection are directed to stock, others will go directly into inbound value-added processing.
- Sortation. Where product inspection or counting is required, the product is moved from the receiving area to an inspection/sortation workstation. At that workstation, the product is inspected, credit is

---

[10] Disposition, in this context, defines the facility the product is to be returned to. It may include return direct to the original manufacturer, return to the shipping warehouse or another company facility such as a central return center, or return to a third-party location.

issued (if not already done), and the product is dispositioned. Available dispositions include restock, rework, scrap, salvage, and hold. Where rework is required, management-defined rules allow the operator to define and generate a work order for the processes required[11].
- Aggregation. Depending on disposition, sorted product can be aggregated in a holding area until an efficient lot size is accumulated. Management rules determine the required lot size and limit on-shelf time.
- Processing. Product released for processing is accompanied by a work order (which may be physical or can be electronic). Movements between workstations are RF controlled and completions at the workstations are tracked. Workstation inventory of supply and point-of-use items can be controlled and tracked using either a bill of material or a usage rate table and normal warehouse management system replenishment processes can be used to refill these stocks as needed. Work order priority (and thus movement priority) is determined by management rules and/or by need for the product in the warehouse.
- Returnables Repository. The warehouse management system maintains a separate repository of returnable containers so that container status and location can be continuously tracked, whether the container is awaiting use in the warehouse, is at a customer site, is in transit, or is being cleaned or repaired. Reports from the repository give management the tools needed to expedite (or invoice for) late returning containers.

The warehouse management system can record actual container numbers (licenses) as containers move through this process, or can count containers by type when licenses are not used. License numbers on reusable containers can be permanent or temporary.

When returns are processed by a third party or at a separate facility, the system can either extend to cover the off-site work, or can treat it as a black box.

- <u>Cycle counting and physical inventory taking.</u> One of the major benefits of a warehouse management system is an increase in the accuracy of inventory records, often to the point where physical inventory taking is no longer required and where less-costly cycle counting will satisfy both auditors and customers. Some industries, however, are required by regulation to perform physicals and some companies simply prefer them. Warehouse management systems, therefore, usually support both cycle counting and physical inventories.

---

[11] The logic applies to containers as well as product.

The cycle counting and physical inventory processes are closely related and usually work from common software. Features normally provided include:

- The ability to schedule counts from a desktop based on specific locations, product characteristics, or location characteristics,
- The ability to automatically schedule counts based on inventory quantity trigger points (when locations are empty or nearly empty) or pick exceptions. Automatic count scheduling can also consider item activity and other item characteristics.
- The ability to "cascade" counts from a location found to be in error to all other locations in the warehouse containing that product.
- RF direction of cycle counters and real-time updating of inventories
- Escalation of counts where errors are found to higher levels of authority (supervisors) when quantity or value thresholds are exceeded.
- Optional blind counting based on management rules. Either the item identity or the quantity on hand or both can be withheld from the counter to assure that the product is actually identified and counted.
- Count methods sensitive to location quantities and packaging and to counter vehicles. Sealed cartons and wrapped pallets, for instance, need only be counted while locations containing open cartons and loose pieces must be counted at the each level.
- Most warehouse management systems allow counting to be restricted to individuals who are specially trained, or to be mixed with other work as the opportunity presents itself.

➢ <u>Cross-docking.</u> Cross-docking is the movement of material directly from receiving to shipping without ever putting it away or picking it. While potentially a significant labor savings, the processes can be complex and often violate stock rotation rules.

Cross-docking takes different forms for businesses that push product to customers vs. those that pull[12]. When product is pushed out the door, shipping schedules are determined by the warehouse and thus can be adjusted to match receipts. This means that a much larger percentage of the material handled can be cross-docked and that cross-docking can be a much larger percentage of the business. The more common pull process requires shipment to a customer's schedule, which usually means that the opportunity to cross-dock is limited to two instances: (1) when product due for shipment happens to arrive at or almost at the same time, and (2) when product is out of stock and shipment is delayed pending receipt.

---

[12] Push distribution is common in retail and relatively rare elsewhere. In push distribution, the warehouse (or a central agency) decides what customers – or which stores – receives what product at what time. In pull distribution, the individual customers determine what product they need and when it should be shipped.

When push distribution is in use and when large amounts of product are cross-docked, the term "flow-through" is often applied. Flow-through distribution is simply cross-docking, taken to an extreme.

Cross-docking in a warehouse management system involves two major components: a matching process by which receipts are matched with shipments to determine which arriving piece is to be shipped to which customer and, second, an execution process that directs the operators in the movement of material from receiving to shipping and validates that the work is done correctly.

Typical features of cross-docking processes in most warehouse management systems include:

- The ability to externalize the matching process and download preplanned cross-dock movements from a host computer. This feature is particularly relevant in the retail industry, which commonly uses a "registration" process through which product buyers predetermine which stores receive what products. Some warehouse management systems are able to entirely replace inbound (purchase) orders and outbound (customer) orders with a registration database.
- An internal, opportunistic matching process that examines inbound material, compares it to planned shipments, and automatically schedules cross-dock movements. This process often can be based either on actual receipts, running in real time as receipts are recorded, or can plan based on expected inbound orders.
- Allocation rules that guide the internal matching process when product arriving is insufficient to fill all orders. These rules also govern the system's response to unexpected receiving shortages or to inbound damage and quality problems.
- A manual planning process through which users can individually specify needed cross-docks.
- A sortation system interface as part of the receiving process. This interface allows arriving cartons to be simply placed on a conveyor and automatically routed to the appropriate shipping door.
- The ability to stage products in shipping pending the arrival of the appropriate trailer and the ability to control loading from that staging location via RF.
- The ability to exempt products and customers from cross-docking, often because of stock rotation requirements.
- The ability to override product/customer exemptions when product arrives that is out of stock (when there are no stock rotation issues).

- Warehouse and inventory management functions are a necessary addition to the basics.

    o Warehouse management systems are almost always able to track product by license plate[13]. License plates are generally nestable (one license can contain others). Transactions can be executed at various levels of a nested license.
    o Product weights and dimensions are maintained and transactions can be executed at various levels of packaging (pallet, carton, inner pack, each, etc.)
    o Multiple units of measure are supported and used appropriately, both on inbound and outbound orders and as product is handled.
    o Material hazards are identified and tracked including UN numbers, primary and subsidiary classes, and other identifying information. Hazard codes are used to control handling, storage and transportation of the product.
    o Product country of origin can be captured from inbound orders or at receiving time, is tracked as product moves through the warehouse, and can be used to control picking when customer orders require it.
    o Material ownership (including material on consignment) can be captured from inbound orders or at receiving time and is tracked as product moves through the warehouse. Ownership change can be supported and ownership can be used in the determination of which product to pick for which order.
    o Holds are provided on material and on storage locations. Material holds prevent picking and shipment and can trigger movement to a quality or inspection function, while location holds allow picking, but prevent storage in the location. Multiple holds on a location, item or license plate are supported, with the most restrictive hold establishing the rules.
    o Duty-paid status can be captured from inbound orders or at receiving time and is tracked as product moves through the warehouse. Duty status can be used in the determination of which product to pick for which order and the export of duty-paid product can trigger automatic drawback records. This capability is an essential part of operation in a foreign trade zone.
    o Manufacturer's lot numbers can be captured from inbound orders or at receiving time and can be tracked as product moves through the warehouse. Multiple lot numbers are allowed for assembled product. Product age can be a function of lot numbering and (usually with custom coding) can be determined by parsing the lot number itself. Outbound orders can specify a required lot number.

---

[13] A license plate is a unique serial number assigned to a material handling unit such as a pallet or a carton. Some systems support only single-item licenses, but the best support mixed items on a license.

- Product age is captured either from inbound orders or ASNs or at receiving time and is tracked as product moves through the warehouse. Product age is used as the basis of stock rotation. FIFO and LIFO rotation rules are both supported.
- Product expiration is calculated from product age and shelf life specifications. Shelf life can be based on the product or the customer and can include an allowance for transportation time. Expired product is automatically placed on hold, but authorized users can extend the life and remove the hold.
- Product serial numbers can be captured from inbound orders or at receiving time. Some warehouse management systems allow serial numbers to be tracked as product moves through the warehouse, but others re-capture the data as product is picked and shipped. In some circumstances, re-capture is more efficient that tracking.
- Warehouse management systems almost always include the ability for a user to update license plate numbers, weights and dimensions, units of measure, material hazards, countries of origin, ownership, hold status, duty status, lot numbers product age, expiration status, and serial numbers as needed. These updates are intended primarily for error-correction purposes.
- Tools allow users to update inventories, products, and locations individually or in groups by lot number, hold status, material hazard, country of origin, ownership, duty status, or expiration status.
- A system tool allows the manual adjustment of inventory, usually including reason and responsibility codes.
- Users are allowed to specify inventory relocation within the warehouse, either designating specific source and destination locations, or allowing allocation and/or putaway rules to be used. These relocations can be specified before the product is moved – in which case the system prioritizes, directs, and validates the movement – or after the fact, simply for recordkeeping purposes.
- Most warehouse management systems provide shortcut ways for authorized users to remove inventory from the warehouse (for example, taking a sample from stock for a salesperson). These shortcuts allow the user to specify the product and quantity and then direct a material handler via RF to retrieve the product and deliver it to the requestor. The transactions are, of course, logged.

- Labor management and labor metrics. Most warehouse management systems include at least a rudimentary way of measuring the performance of individuals and groups in the warehouse. Performance measurement can be an important motivational tool; anecdotal reports often claim increases in performance of as much as 25%, simply by the implementation of the measurement. The best labor management functions include:

  - A transaction history that tracks all transactions, recording the operator's ID, several characteristics of the work done, and starting and ending date and time stamps
  - The ability to base performance measures on a variety of measures starting with simple transaction counting and proceeding to highly sophisticated time standards.
  - Time standards that are dynamically calculated for each task and each task group (work assignment). These engineered time standards can optionally be a function of the type of work, the zone in which the work is done, the travel distance required, the type and speed of the vehicle in use, the quantity, packaging and weight of the material handled, the type of material handled, the type of storage device(s) in use, and the time required for data entry and for any supporting paper work.
  - The ability to optionally calculate standard times based on historical records of actual performance.
  - Tools and options that allow users to trade off setup complexity for precision in the standard time calculations. For example, users can choose between simple zone-to-zone travel distance determination and a complex and data-intensive, 3-dimensional location-to-location calculation.
  - Tools that allow users to determine whether individuals or workgroups are to be measured and, in the latter case, that allow the makeup of work groups to change from time to time.
  - Either an internal time and attendance system or integration with third-party systems. These systems include the ability to track time and attendance data for indirect and clerical workers as well as for pickers, lift-truck drivers, etc.
  - An interface capable of transmitting a variety of labor data (including time and attendance data) to a payroll system.
  - RF and/or workstation functionality that allows individual operators to check their productivity measurement in real time at any point during the day.
  - Optional goal presentation, in which the individual operators are told in advance what the time standard is for the work they are about to do, so they have a goal to strive for[14].

---

[14] There are obvious disadvantages to giving operators this information if standard times are not precise and accurate. Goal presentation, therefore, is almost always a management option.

- Performance reports and graphical analysis at the operator, work group, department and facility level.
- Tools (primarily event logs and reporting mechanisms) that support disciplinary action.
- Tools that allow the evaluation of time standards elements based on accumulated actual experience.
- The ability to apply standard times to unplanned work and thus predict labor requirements by zone, department, type of work, and other criteria. (Unplanned work is work for which detailed material movements have not yet been determined. It normally cannot be evaluated using the same standards calculations as performance measurement.)
- The ability to apply standard times to forecast work and thus see and analyze a longer-term projection of labor requirements. (Forecast work is work for which orders have not yet been received. Order forecasts are similar to sales forecasts, but more detailed.)

➢ <u>Yard Management.</u> Yard management systems manage the space between the warehouse walls and the fence, tracking the inventory of trailers and controlling trailer movement. Yard management systems are, in effect, simplified warehouse management systems with features customized for the purpose. This paper considers the yard management function to be an integral part of the warehouse management system, but many yard management systems are able to run standalone and many software suppliers consider yard management to be separate.

Almost all yard management systems handle straight trucks, trailers and ocean containers with equal ease. Few, if any, include the features necessary to efficiently manage a rail yard.

Important features in most yard management systems include:

- An appointment calendar and the ability to schedule appointments for incoming and outgoing freight. Scheduling is usually supported either by phone/fax contact with the carrier (and manual data entry) and/or via the Internet.
- The capture of trailer content either via EDI or via data entry from a bill of lading. Capture can occur either in advance or at trailer arrival time
- Automatic calculation of unloading time (dwell time) estimates for scheduling purposes
- A trailer arrival function, usually staffed either by a guard at the warehouse gate or by a clerk in the warehouse transportation office. The arrival function checks in arriving trailers, can validate seals, and can capture driver ID, trailer ID and tractor ID. The arrival function also identifies dropped trailers separately from live loads (if not defined

earlier), notes trailer defects, and identifies trailers by type (flatbed, dry van, reefer, etc.[15]) and size.
- The ability to assign arriving trailers either to docks/doors or to parking spaces. The assignment routine includes consideration of dock/door availability and suitability for the trailer type as well as the need for the product on the trailer.
- Trailer space assignment capabilities usually include the ability to handle multiple yards and the distinction between local and remote yards.
- Trailer status is tracked while the trailer is on the property. This tracking includes status (loaded and intended for empty departure, loaded for reloading, empty for pickup, empty for loading, loaded for pickup), driver status (waiting or dropped), a listing of known trailer defects and safety hazards, the length of time the trailer has been on the property, calculation of demurrage charges, and a measure of the degree to which the original appointment was kept by the carrier.
- The yard management system initiates and controls movements within the yard and to and from the docks. Movements are initiated through a priority scheme that considers the need for the material on the trailer (inbound) or the need for the trailer itself (outbound) as well as dock/door availability and other factors. Live loads are usually given some priority over drops; demurrage charges are usually considered for dropped trailers. Drivers who kept their appointments and are now waiting are usually given priority over those who were late (or early).
- Movement is controlled either using a yard jockey with an RF terminal (for trailer drops) or using the over-the-road driver (for live loads). Some systems provide optional contact with over-the-road drivers through a pager that is given to drivers on arrival and returned on departure.
- A departure function controls the departure of trailers. This function usually includes the verification of seals, driver ID, tractor ID and trailer ID, a safety check, and sometimes a weight check.
- Most yard management systems also include the ability to take a simple physical inventory of the yard and the ability to manually adjust yard inventory including both trailer identities and locations.
- The better yard management systems also are able to interface with external owned fleet systems (such as driver assignment systems, preventive maintenance systems, etc.) and with carrier systems.

---

[15] Few systems are designed to deal appropriately with bulk trailers or tankers.

➢ Task Interleaving. Most warehouse operators do one kind of work at a time: receiving, putaway, replenishing, picking, packing, shipping, etc. Task interleaving is the ability to assign multiple kinds of work to an operator, with individual task assignments made depending, at least in part, on proximity. If, for instance, a person doing putaways happens to put away a pallet that is close to a pallet that is scheduled to be picked, he or she might be directed to do the pick and deliver it to the shipping dock before doing the next putaway. The objective is to reduce unloaded travel and thus reduce labor cost.

Warehouse management system interleaving functions usually include the ability to:

- Limit interleaving to selected types of work and selected areas (zones) in the warehouse
- Consider work priority as part of the interleaving decision
- Limit interleaving to selected personnel (presumably the more experienced workers)
- Limit interleaving based on the type of load handled (pallet, carton, etc.) and on the vehicle in use

➢ Management overview, analysis and reporting. Warehouse management systems maintain very large and detailed databases and extensive history files. This data can be a gold mine of management information for the warehouse manager and for other senior management. The warehouse management system therefore supports a variety of management tools including:

- General-purpose analytical and reporting tools, capable of selecting, sorting, summarizing and presenting data as needed. These tools almost always include graphic reporting functions.
- The on-line ability to track the progress of orders, waves, inventories, operators, vehicles, and space in real time.
- Warehouse facility profiles and system configuration critiques
- Event management functions including configurable alarms and alerts that can be transmitted via email, pager, fax and/or telephone to wherever the manager is.

➢ Activity Based Costing. Activity based costing is a method of determining product cost in which indirect costs are tracked, recorded and valued in detail, rather than being allocated as overhead. While few warehouse management systems (if any) contain complete activity based costing systems as built-in features, most capture and record significant data that can be used elsewhere in product costing, whether the costing function is activity based or more traditional.

- Other functions. The best warehouse management systems also include a variety of miscellaneous functions and features:

    - The ability to assign and adjust order priorities
    - User-configurable functions that automatically substitute product to compensate for out-of-stock conditions[16].
    - A function that allows operators and supervisors to exchange text messages via RF terminals
    - Multi-lingual capabilities that allow (1) individual users to select a language of choice and then communicate with the system in that language and (2) packing lists and other shipping paper to be produced in the customer or carrier's language of choice.
    - Unit of measure functions that allow customers to order in one unit (e.g., a measure of weight) and warehouse operators to work in another unit (e.g., pieces). These same functions can rationalize units of measure for the operators so that if a customer orders 75 pieces of a product that is packaged in dozens, the operator is directed to pick 6 cartons and three pieces, rather than requiring him or her to do the math.
    - The ability to display product photographs and/or detailed product descriptions to material handlers as a way of minimizing incorrect item picks
    - The ability to break material moves into multiple steps to accommodate different vehicles. This includes, for instance, the hand-off of a putaway from a conventional lift truck to a high-rise crane.
    - A function that allows product to be reserved for a specific customer and manages the allocation of product that is in short supply among numerous competing customers. This function usually works with management-defined rules and is usually capable of acting at the customer level, the sales rep level, or the sales region level.
    - Functions that manage leased pallets and that work with pallet exchange programs
    - Vender managed inventory (VMI) functions allowing inbound orders to be received from suppliers and, in some cases, allowing supplier personnel to perform the receiving and putaway functions.
    - Order and inventory status visibility (via secure Internet functions), both for internal departments and external entities such as customers and suppliers.
    - Walk-in functions that combine basic retail point-of-sale capabilities with the warehouse management system to support an on-site public store. Features include order entry, real-time product allocation, RF-

---

[16] Substitution is probably best done at the CRM level, but is available in many warehouse management systems to accommodate instances in which the host is unable to substitute and instances of last-minute quality problems or unanticipated shortages.

directed picking for items not stocked in the retail area, pricing, and invoice/receipt printing[17].
- Interfaces to external shipment tracking web sites
- Check-digit validation of material handling moves. This function associates check digits with locations and requires their entry in place of location bar code scans. It is useful when bar code location labeling is not physically possible, as with open floor storage, inside some freezers, in an outdoor storage yard, etc.
- A variety of user-defined data fields on the database and in communications layouts. These fields can be assigned unique meanings for a specific installation without software customization and can generally be used to impact processes such as stock allocation, pick priority, item slotting, carrier selection and more. User-defined fields should be included on the item table, both inbound and outbound orders (at both the header and detail levels), the bill-of-material, the customer and supplier tables, the location table, and in a number of other places.
- Optional functions capable of producing item labels and directing their application at receipt time
- The ability to generate outbound ASNs at shipment time.
- The ability to manage a bank of printers in high-volume printing operations. This management should include workload distribution across the printers in the bank and accommodation of printer failures.

---

[17] Pre-ordered customer pickups are generally handled with other shipping functions. In most systems, the customer is simply designated as another carrier.

Industry-Specific Function and Feature

Some industry groups have need for function and feature in a warehouse management system that goes beyond standard capabilities. These extensions are sometimes driven simply by industry experience and tradition, but other times arise from special safety concerns and/or government regulations.

Although historically industry-specific, these functions and features can be useful outside of their intended industry. Management in all industries should familiarize themselves with at least the basic outlines of these items as a source of ideas.

- Lot and serial number control, commonly found in the food and beverage, pharmaceutical, electronics, industrial equipment businesses. Complete lot and serial number tracking includes the ability to

    - Capture and track lot and serial numbers as product arrives, moves through the warehouse, and is shipped.
    - Accept and properly handle orders for a specific lot number or serial number
    - Document shipment by customer and manage product recalls if and when they occur

- Product expiration, commonly found in the food and beverage and pharmaceutical industries. Product expiration capabilities are sometimes tied into lot and serial number control with the ability to decode a lot number to determine the date of manufacture and thus the date of product expiration. Features include the ability to:

    - Calculate expiration dates from manufacture dates
    - Rotate stock based on expiration date rather than warehouse receipt date
    - Accept and manage customer orders for a specified level of freshness (i.e., time to expiration)
    - Place holds on product automatically when expiration occurs, thereby preventing shipment of expired product
    - Prevent shipment of product that will be expired or which will have less than a minimum shelf life remaining by the time it reaches the customer.
    - Maintain strict expiration date sequencing by customer

Selecting, Buying, Installing and Using a Modern Warehouse Management System

- Style/size/color. In the apparel and footwear industries, some companies assign style numbers to items and append size and color numbers to denote variations on the style. In these instances, the complete SKU or item number is generally composed of the style, size and color numbers combined. Good management of style/size/color information requires the ability to:

    o Define substitution rules for sizes and colors within a style
    o Automatically build assortments (see below) for a style based on a standard size/color distribution.
    o Locate stock based on style to minimize picker travel
    o Report at the style, size, color or SKU/item levels

- Grade. Apparel and footwear businesses also sometimes maintain a product grade (firsts, seconds, etc.) that works much like style, size and color.

- Assortments. Apparel and footwear firms also frequently deal with assortments, sometimes called "musicals" in the footwear business. Assortment management requires that the warehouse management system be capable of:

    o Defining assortment content by style or style group
    o Generating work transactions to pick individual SKUs or items, deliver them to a packing station for creation of the assortments, movement of the completed work back to stock, and subsequent handling of the material under an assortment number.
    o Determining (usually with management approval) when disassembly of a stocked assortment is needed to recover an individual SKU or item, and management of the material handling work required
    o Reporting at the assortment (stocking) level or at the individual SKU/item level.

- Hazardous materials. A surprising number of warehouses handle materials classified as DOT hazards, although many have only a few hazardous items in stock. Hazardous material functions in warehouse management systems were originally developed for the chemical and pharmaceutical industries, but often can be of significant value in bringing a warehouse with limited hazards into full compliance with regulations and standards. Features available in the better warehouse management systems include:

    o Ability to issue safety warnings to employees when they handle hazardous materials including instructions for the use of proper protective equipment

- Ability to segregate certain hazards in separate storage facilities[18]
- Ability to enforce special storage rules that limit the proximity of different hazards in storage and/or the amount of a specific hazard that can be stored in a single location or within a certain distance of another hazard
- Requirements for packaging inspection at receipt time
- Support for shipping requirements of all kinds including carrier notification and carrier prohibitions, special packaging requirements and the printing of various shipping documents.

- Catch weight. The food industry (especially the meat business) sometimes sells product based on weight. The picker, therefore, picks a specific weight without requirement for any particular number of pieces. Because product weight varies over time (largely depending on age and humidity), the amounts received will not neatly reconcile with the amount shipped. The warehouse management system must:

  - Accept orders for a specific weight of product
  - Allow the picker to pick within a tolerance of that weight
  - Usually interface with portable scales and with the calculation of tare weights (pallet weights)
  - Pass the actual weight picked to the host computer for billing purposes.

- Variable product sizes and one-of-a-kind. The furniture industry frequently deals with one-of-a-kind product and with product that has a broad range of sizes. A sofa, for instance, might be anywhere from 48" to 120" long. The warehouse management system should:

  - Maintain dimensional information at the license plate level and allow different pieces of the same SKU or item to have different dimensions
  - Allow dimensional information to either arrive in the system on inbound orders or ASNs, or to be entered at receiving time.
  - Use actual product dimensions in the selection of storage locations for putaway and allow items to occupy portions of (or all of) adjacent locations as necessary.
  - Allow the reservation of a specific piece for a specific customer, even if the order has not yet arrived
  - Intelligently assign lift trucks and other vehicles that can safely handle oversize product

---

[18] This includes the ability to store flammables, for instance, in separate rooms or limit them to sprinkler-equipped racks.

- Wire, cable and cut-to-length items. The hardware industry and some manufacturers deal with reels of wire, chain, and cable; and have items like pipe or rod or bar stock that must be cut to length; the furniture industry deals with carpet that is also cut to length. To handle cut-to-length items properly, the warehouse management system must be able to:

    - Pre-assign picks to reels or lengths that are efficient for cutting to minimize remainders. This usually means assigning a specific pick to the one reel or length that is the shortest-but-long-enough.
    - Simultaneously deal with customer specified lot numbers (to assure color matching when necessary)
    - Manage the material handling and bench work required to move the reel/length to a cutting station, perform the cut, and return the remainder to stock.
    - Deal with the disposal of remainders, usually by recommending that short lengths be scrapped and by managing the scrapping process as recommendations are approved

- 3PL. The third party logistics industry runs warehouses that handle only other firm's products. Warehouse management systems that properly serve 3PLs are capable of:

    - Product ownership tracking in a multi-owner facility
    - Preparing analyses in preparation for customer billing. These analyses usually include considerations of space used (or space reserved for the customer), movements completed, and costs incurred.
    - Preparing other customer analyses such as profitability, stock reports, transaction reports, etc.
    - Providing customized invoicing and bills of lading, different for each customer
    - Passing through accessorial and other charges for customer billing
    - Supporting standard API accounting interfaces

Features and Functions Not Included

Before embarking on a warehouse management system project, it is often useful to understand that some things are generally not provided. The list below briefly discusses things that you might think would make sense in a warehouse management system, but which are rarely (if ever) included as internal function.

- Transportation. Transportation management functions are complex enough to have demanded development efforts entirely separate from warehouse management systems and thus, today, appear in the market as separate systems. These functions are surprisingly broad, including:

    o Network design
    o Carrier contracting
    o Spot purchase
    o Route design
    o Rating and routing
    o Manifesting/BOL preparation
    o Inbound planning
    o Carrier scheduling
    o Loading planning
    o Carrier compliant labeling
    o Vehicle maintenance and management
    o Operator (driver) management
    o International trade
    o Emergency services
    o Vehicle location monitoring
    o Carrier analysis
    o Freight bill audit, payment and accounting
    o Claim management
    o Operator (driver) relations and compensation
    o Duty management
    o Regulatory monitoring

    Although warehouse management systems almost never include integral transportation functions, virtually all of them do include well-tested interfaces and many suppliers resell transportation management systems provided by other firms.

- Equipment maintenance. The maintenance and management of warehouse machinery including lift trucks, conveyors and all manner of handling and storage equipment would seem to be a natural extension to a warehouse management system. Demand for these functions, however, has not been significant and so system suppliers have not seen adequate payback to justify the development cost. As a result, warehouses that need help with equipment preventive maintenance, spare part inventories, and replacement analyses will have to buy separately and any required integration with the warehouse management system will likely become a separate project.

➢ <u>Pallet and load configuration.</u> In businesses that build mixed pallets, there can be significant gains in transportation when the pallets are built correctly to minimize product damage and maximize the use of the space on the pallet. A closely related problem can arise with the loading of trailers where the management of axle loading and, sometimes, the need to accommodate multiple stops and easy offloading ads to the complexity.

Systems exist that can work from the geometry of the items to be loaded on either a pallet or a trailer, calculate the optimum loading pattern, and direct workers in the construction of the load. Demand for these functions, however, has been small, particularly because need is relatively uncommon and the process of efficiently communicating an optimum pattern to the people doing the loading is difficult. Further, development costs are high because the work is very complex. Warehouse system suppliers, therefore, have not invested in load configuration or load building function. Businesses that need help in this area will again be faced with a separate system purchase and an integration project.

In addition, as previously noted, systems that design and manage the re-slotting of a warehouse are sometimes integral to the warehouse management system, but at other times are separate.

WMS Costs and Benefits

The possible range of cost and benefit for a warehouse management system is very large. It depends heavily on the system being considered, the current, pre-installation state of the warehouse, the size and complexity of the operation, the amount of customization needed and many other factors.

Once all project costs have been estimated, totals are likely to begin at about $200,000 for the smallest and simplest warehouse and can run anywhere from there up to several million dollars for the most complex. Primary cost determinants include:

- Size and complexity of the warehouse
- Size and complexity of the supply chain
- Number of operators to be trained and equipped
- Number of transactions to be processed daily
- System features required
- Amount of customization required
- Economic clout of the buying organization

Return on investment can run from as little as six months (which is actually rare) to as much as eight or ten years (also rare). There are no rules of thumb that can reliably tell us in advance whether a warehouse management system will be a wise investment. Only detailed analysis, well beyond the scope of this paper, is sufficient to do that. We can, however, outline typical system costs and the sources of typical system benefits as a starting point for analysis.

Both costs and benefits come in several varieties: there are one-time and recurring costs and benefits as well as tangible and intangible ones. Although analysts sometimes tend to concentrate on the tangibles, it is important that the intangibles be considered as well since they often will make or break project justification. (They can also make or break an installation project.)

Although on-demand (or hosted) warehouse management systems are available, they are an extremely small part of the market and are not likely to become a major force in the foreseeable future. This discussion, therefore, assumes the purchase of a software license and the operation of the system on company-owned servers.

ERP Systems vs. Best-of-Breed

The warehouse management system industry tends to separate those systems from enterprise requirements planning system suppliers (ERP systems) from those supplied by independent firms (best-of-breed systems). In general,

> ➢ ERP warehouse management systems offer truly seamless integration with many other business systems, a single point of support for multiple elements of software, and sometimes lower license fees.

> ➢ Best of breed systems, on the other hand, often offer richer feature sets and personnel who better understand supply chain and warehousing issues and problems. Further, best of breed suppliers are generally more experienced and have a better grasp of special and unusual requirements and they are often better at interfacing their systems to material handling equipment and other non-ERP software such as transportation management systems.

The choice between an ERP and a best-of-breed warehouse management system differs little from the choice between any other two systems. Both should be evaluated and the system that makes the best overall economic sense should be chosen. We, therefore, do not treat the decision separately, but integrate it entirely in to the discussions presented.

Hardware and Infrastructure Costs

Modern warehouse management systems almost exclusively follow the client-server model, with the system itself running on one or more central servers and connected to users through a network of clients.

Servers

Servers typically run Microsoft Windows or UNIX/LINUX, but a small number of AS400 applications are also available on the market. The number and size of the servers required is mostly a function of the size and throughput volume of the warehouse(s) to be supported, but also varies from warehouse management system to system.

Some warehouse management systems are capable of supporting multiple warehouses on a single server instance; others require a dedicated server for each warehouse. However, while it may sound like a good idea to minimize hardware investment by running multiple warehouses on a single box, there are drawbacks. Possibly the most significant argument for dedicated servers is the fact that the warehouses are thus isolated from each other; a surge in volume at one site will thus not affect response times across the corporate network.

The only reliable way to determine server equipment cost is to ask the warehouse management system supplier for a quote. Most suppliers have sizing worksheets that, when filled in with a client's volume statistics, will define the number and size of servers required. Quite a few suppliers are able and often eager to resell hardware and will provide a detailed quotation and, possibly, even warrant performance.

Figure 4. Typical hand-held portable terminal

Clients

In addition to servers, the warehouse management system requires client workstations. Essentially all workstations today are simple desktop PCs with browser interfaces into the system. Existing PCs can normally be used but if computing power is to be provided in locations where there has been none, new PCs may be required.

Figure 5. Typical vehicle-mount portable terminal

Portable terminals

The essence of a modern warehouse management system is in real-time computing and remote portable access for operators. This requires a wireless network in the warehouse and compatible wireless terminals for most warehouse operators.

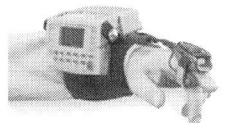

Figure 6. Typical wearable terminal and bar code scanner

Wireless data terminals come in three basic designs: the hand-held, the vehicle mount, and the "wearable," all illustrated at the right[19].

The cost of a wireless network covering the entire warehouse can be significant and can approach the cost of the warehouse management system license itself.

Figure 7. Typical wireless voice terminal in use

Cost is generally a function of the features needed and the number of users. Features available from most manufacturers include:

---

[19] Illustrations are courtesy of Symbol Technologies, Inc. They are presented here as examples and not as an endorsement of Symbol Technologies or its products.

- Varying screen sizes and graphics capabilities
- Varying keyboard layouts ranging from full QWERTY keyboards to simple numeric keypads with function keys
- Varying duty cycles between battery changes; varying battery charge cycles
- Laser bar code readers and/or RFID scanners either integrated into the terminal or cable-connected; both long and short range scanning supported
- Support for portable label printing
- Integrated voice connectivity, usually in a walkie-talkie mode
- Intrinsically safe units for use with a variety of hazardous materials and in other hazardous circumstances
- Thermally protected units for use in freezers and harsh environments
- A wide variety of holsters, harnesses, straps, vehicle mounts and other accessories.

In some instances, with appropriate supporting software, wireless voice terminals can replace data terminals with significant productivity gains. Voice terminals use speech recognition software to covert the operator's spoken commands into character strings for the warehouse management system, and use voice synthesis to provide him or her with audible feedback. They have the advantage of leaving the operator's hands and eyes free and since most people can easily speak or listen and perform work at the same time, they have significant potential for increasing productivity. However, voice terminals can present issues for speech or hearing-impaired workers and they sometimes have difficulty handling background noise, especially around automated material handling equipment.

Voice terminals, when properly configured, also have the interesting property of being language-free. In other words, they can be set up to communicate with each user that that user's choice of language, almost without limitation. This can be of significant value in warehouses where multiple languages are spoken and especially when there is no single common language.

When estimating requirements, include several spares, especially for hand-held units. Regardless of how ruggedly they are built, damage will occur, so extra units are needed to cover for those sent out for repair.

RF connectivity can be either impossible or uneconomic in a few situations such as large outdoor storage yards or in warehouses that contain large amounts of grounded metal that prevents RF propagation. And, at times, the cost of RF is simply too great and the entire project justification suffers. To accommodate these situations, some warehouse management systems are also able to work with portable batch-oriented terminals, illustrated at the right[20].

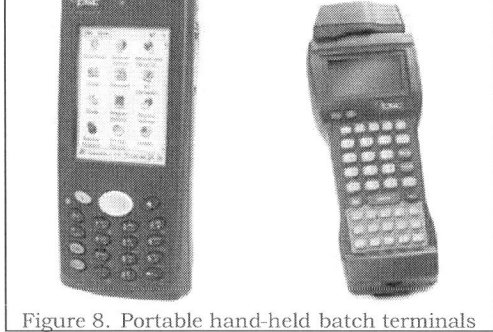

Figure 8. Portable hand-held batch terminals

Batch terminals have two basic advantages over RF: they will work anywhere, and they are much less expensive because they eliminate the need for the radio network. However, the use of batch terminals also eliminates the advantages of a real-time system and thus can significantly reduce the benefits of the WMS.

Fixed-location bar code/RFID scanners

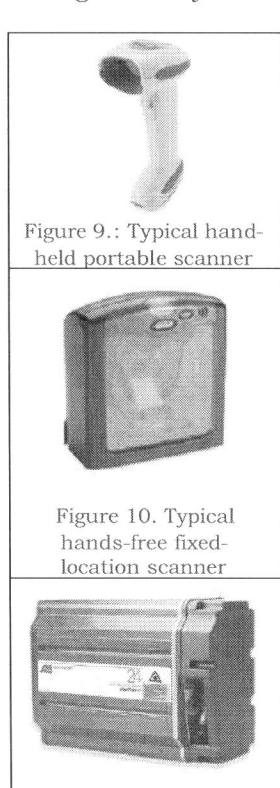

Almost all warehouse management systems make extensive use of bar codes and some systems in some situations use RFID to either supplement or replace some bar codes. Most bar code scanning is done through portable RF or batch terminals, but warehouses that make significant use of RFID and those that have automation may also need fixed-location scanners. In addition, warehouses that do significant amounts of bench work (often value added services) may need additional fixed-location scanners.

Figure 9.: Typical hand-held portable scanner

Figure 10. Typical hands-free fixed-location scanner

The simplest fixed-location bar code scanners are connected to a PC in parallel with the keyboard using a device called a "wedge." They are manually operated and inexpensive. More complex units connect directly to a network or to a PC through a USB port. Still more complex units run continuously and read bar codes as an operator presents them. These continuous operation units may best be applied at packing stations or other instances where volume is significant and the extra cost of the units is justified by eliminating the need for the operator to trigger the scan[21].

Figure 11. Typical automated barcode scanner

---

[20] Illustrations are courtesy of PSC, Inc. They are presented here as examples and not as an endorsement of PSC or its products.
[21] Illustrations are courtesy of Symbol Technologies Inc. and Accu-Sort Systems Inc. They are presented here as examples and not as an endorsement of Symbol, Accu-Sort, or their products.

Still more sophisticated and powerful scanners operate continuously and can read labels on product passing on a conveyor, regardless of the orientation of the label to the scanner. These devices are often coupled to sensors that detect the presence of an object on the conveyor and generally feed the information collected into a special-purpose conveyor control system that determines how to sort the object based on information in the bar code.

The conveyor control system may subsequently pass the information back to a warehouse management system.

Bar code/RFID printers

The cost of bar code printing has dropped dramatically over the last ten years and today almost all inexpensive windows-compatible printers are capable of producing useable bar codes on documents like packing lists and bills of lading. The printing of labels, however, is limited to sheet-fed label stock in most windows printers, so many companies continue to use special-purpose label printers that use roll stock and are capable of printing one label at a time.[22]

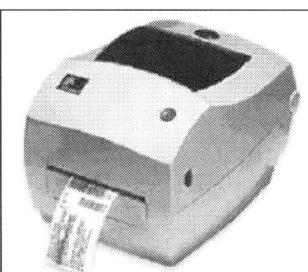

Figure 12. Typical bar code label printer

Label printers usually use either direct thermal or thermal transfer technology. RFID label printers use label stock with RFID tags embedded in the paper stock. They print the label and encode the RFID tag simultaneously.

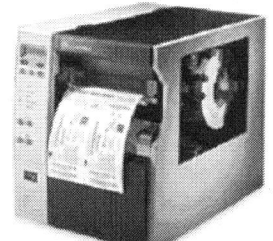

Figure 13. Typical RFID label printer

For high-volume carton labeling, many companies use printer-applicators, capable of automatically producing a label and applying it to a carton. These devices are, of course, only useable when there is a way of providing the printer with the information needed to go on the label and this, at times, can be problematic.

Figure 14. Typical label printer/ applicator

---

[22] Illustrations are courtesy of Zebra Technologies Corp. and Accu-Sort Systems Inc. They are presented here as examples and not as an endorsement of Zebra, Accu-Sort, or their products.

Networks

Warehouse management systems use networks to join components of the system such as servers, clients, printers, and RF base stations. Most companies installing a warehouse management system can use an existing network, but large businesses with significant network traffic may wish to consider a separate network for the warehouse management system to assure high speeds and to eliminate possible delay.

The warehouse management system supplier can assist with estimates of network traffic.

Supplementary software

Warehouse management systems are generally not complete within themselves, but require supplementary software to function. Users should expect to separately license (and purchase support) for:

- Operating systems (windows, UNIX, etc.)
- A database manager
- A report writer and possibly separate label printing software
- Data analysis and data warehousing tools

The operating system and database manager can be significant expenses, so they should be carefully researched as part of any warehouse management system project.

Site preparation

Site preparation requirements for warehouse management systems are generally minimal, at least when compared with the installation of material handling equipment. However, any or all of the following may be needed:

- Data or networking cables may need to be installed or extended to new locations (especially for RF base stations)
- Electrical power may need to be provided in new locations for client PCs, printers, and RF base stations
- Workstation and printer space (including power and data connections) may be needed where none existed before
- Lift trucks may require modification to provide power for vehicle-mounted RF terminals
- Space (and power) must be provided for RF terminal battery charging stations
- Storage space will be needed for supplies, especially label stock

Software Costs

Strictly speaking, firms do not purchase warehouse management systems, but only purchase licenses to use them. Such licenses are normally perpetual and include a copy of the executable code. Perpetual support, of course, is not included and must be purchased separately.

There have been instances in which users have negotiated for copies of the system's source code, delivered under a special license. Source code can be used in one of two ways:

- o Under seal (or in escrow), it can serve as backup for the user company, insulating it in the event of business failure or other default on the part of the suppler
- o When not sealed, a copy of the source code can allow the user company to make its own software modifications and do software support internally. One should, of course, expect to pay for the rights to the source code. Significant IT skills and extensive programmer training are both required.

Licensing provides the user with the rights to execute the code. Licenses, as contractual documents, are flexible. They almost always limit the user to operation of the system in its own business and may also limit operation in other ways. It is common for licenses to specify a maximum number of simultaneous users allowed[23] and some licenses also limit system operation in other ways (for example, transaction counts). These limits are sometimes enforced in the software, but more often are simply contractual.

Most warehouse management systems are structured into a base package plus add-on functional modules. Of course, fees increase as more modules are licensed. License fees for the base package can run from a low of about $3,000 for a tier-3 system to a high of $250,000 for a tier-1 system. Add-on module pricing varies even more widely, so the package sold to a specific user can range from as little as a few thousand dollars to as much as a half-million or more. Of course, one gets what one pays for in terms of system feature, function and quality.

Although warehouse system suppliers have standard pricing for their modules, essentially all are simply starting points for negotiation. The user who simply accepts a supplier's fee without asking for a reduction is leaving money on the table.

---

[23] When dealing with suppliers, be sure you understand how users are counted; sometimes RF users are counted individually and sometimes only the RF base station is counted as a user.

Other Project Costs

Hardware, infrastructure and software costs are only the most visible cost elements in a warehouse management system installation project. For a complete cost picture – which is essential to a good system selection project and to accurate project justification – a number of other costs must be considered.

Customization

Essentially all warehouse management system suppliers are in the business of customizing their software to meet the needs of an individual user company. Customization not only represents a source of revenue for the supplier, it also provides continuing revenue since there are also charges for ongoing support of the customizations.

Customization of a warehouse management system is not necessarily either good or bad. However, neither entry into a system selection process with the idea that the software will be used as-is, nor with the idea that the software must exactly match existing business practices and must meet all user requirements from the start are probably not good ideas. Each individual change to a supplier's software should, instead, be justified on its own merits.

The primary drivers of customization are interfaces (discussed below), business and industry practices that depart from existing software features, and regulation. In some instances customization is mandatory, particularly when government regulation is the driver. One example might be the firearms industry, regulated by the Federal Treasury Department's Bureau of Alcohol, Tobacco and Firearms. Another example might be the warehouse that handles nuclear material and is thus regulated by the Nuclear Regulatory Commission. In both instances, product traceability requirements imposed by the government substantially exceed the capabilities of almost all warehouse management systems, but can be handled with customization.

The preferred approach to warehouse customization is in four steps:

1. Determine your goals
2. Invite suppliers to show you how your goals can be reached using their software without software change, but allowing business process change where required
3. Request a quote for the customization
4. Justify the proposed modification by comparing its costs and benefits compared to the supplier's ideas. In this justification, include not only

financial costs, but also system delivery delays since customization will take time to accomplish.

Interfacing

Warehouse management systems rely on connectivity with a broad variety of other business systems both as sources of needed data and as ways of implementing work needed in the warehouse. Interfaces can be implemented to many systems, but are most common with:

- Business hosts, including (but not limited to):
    - Financial systems (general ledger, payables, receivables, payroll. Data is uploaded to these systems as product is received and shipped and as work is accomplished
    - Customer relationship management, sales, order management. Orders are taken from these systems and feedback is provided as shipments are made
    - Purchasing, supplier management, sourcing and merchandising systems. Inbound orders are taken from these systems and feedback is provided as receipts occur
    - Product engineering systems of all kinds. Item information is received from these systems (item information can also be taken from supplier and merchandising systems)
    - Manufacturing Planning Systems. Production schedules provide inbound finished goods warehouse arrival information and outbound information for raw materials and component parts warehouses.
    - Enterprise Resource Planning (ERP) systems. These systems often act as all the others together

- Transportation Management Systems (TMS) include:
    - Parcel manifesting systems
    - Rate shopping and carrier selection systems
    - Fleet and vehicle maintenance and management systems
    - Network design systems
    - Carrier contracting systems
    - Spot purchase systems
    - Route design systems
    - Inbound planning systems
    - Carrier scheduling systems
    - Loading planning systems
    - Operator (driver) management systems
    - International trade systems
    - Emergency services systems
    - Carrier analysis systems
    - Freight bill payment and accounting systems

- Claim management systems
 - Duty management systems
 - Regulatory monitoring systems

- Yard Management Systems (YMS), where these systems are not integral with the warehouse management system

- Material Handling Equipment, most commonly:
  - Carousels
  - Automated storage and retrieval systems (AS/RS)
  - Sortation systems
  - Automated guided vehicles (AGVs)
  - Picking machines (A-frames)

Some warehouse management systems have plug-in capabilities that can be implemented without modification, but these capabilities are generally limited to specific third-party systems and to specific versions of these systems. Other warehouse management systems have "standard generic" interfaces that usually contain some of the infrastructure required, but still require modification to communicate in a specific case.

Most interfaces, therefore, require custom code modifications. Their cost should include interface design, creation (at both ends of the interface) and testing. Interface projects are often done by two organizations, one working at each end of the connection. The need to coordinate the two organizations can sometimes make the project more complex and costly than would otherwise be the case.

Host modifications

Modifications to business hosts can be one of the most significant complications of a warehouse management system installation project. These modifications usually arise for one or both of two reasons:

- Warehouse management systems often use data that is organizationally not the property of the logistics organization (for instance, product weight and dimensions as pieces, in cartons, and on pallets.) Sometimes this information is not available on any business system because it has not been needed in machineable form before. Host extensions are then required to derive or store the needed information where it can best be maintained, and to make it available to the warehouse management system.

- Users of older and legacy host systems often find that the needed interface to a warehouse management system is either not supported or is not adequate. Modification of the host system, of course, is the solution.

There have been instances in which needed host modifications have been larger and more complex than those made to the warehouse management system, in which the host modifications have been more costly than any other single element of the installation project, and in which the host modifications have become the limiting factor in establishing the system go-live date. The time and cost of host modifications and the availability of people with the right skills should be carefully investigated before committing to a project timeline.

System installation and testing

Technical installation of the warehouse management system on the user's server is probably best done at supplier's shop to minimize disruption to the customer's business (this assumes a dedicated server). Installation of the server on site in the customer's location is then a second, but much simpler step.

Some warehouse management system suppliers may charge for server installation, while others include the service in the license fee. Coordinate all installation work with site preparation to the extent required. Also, be sure that the installation will not conflict with daily operations.

Data collection and loading

Following technical installation of the software, the system's tables must be loaded with data, some of which may have to be collected from the real world, while other data may be available for downloading from other systems. The process generally divides into three steps:

> Loading of static data. Static data is data that changes relatively slowly such as item and warehouse location data, employee, supplier and customer tables, etc. Some of this data may exist prior to the warehouse management system project (for example, item data) and be available for import. Other data (such as the location table) may have to be created. Most warehouse management systems provide tools that simplify creation of location tables based, at least in part, on warehouse geometry.
>
> The most difficult and expensive part of the static data loading process is often the establishment of item weights and dimensions. If this data needs to be physically collected on the warehouse floor, it can involve thousands of man-hours to weigh and measure everything. Some warehouse management systems provide workarounds that allow the

measuring job to be spread over a long period of time. Although these workarounds will most likely compromise system benefits during the early months of use, they can allow a much faster and less expensive implementation and should be considered. Remember, however, to consider the cost of the compromised benefits.

Equipment is available that can automatically weigh and measure product, greatly reducing the cost of the startup project and significantly improving the accuracy of the data collected. This equipment is generally available either for purchase or for lease[24].

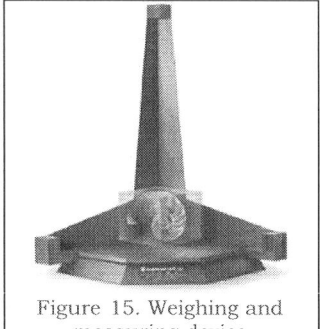

Figure 15. Weighing and measuring device

Finally, it should be noted, that the initial weighing and measuring project can be ideal either for a temporary workforce or for outsourcing (although the work will still need to be done on-site and may require assistance from the user's lift trucks).

- <u>System configuration.</u> Configuration of the warehouse management system consists of establishing initial values for the system's control fields. Included are likely controls that determine zone boundaries, establish worker permissions, determine rules for putaway and the allocation of product for orders, establish product expiration requirements, and possibly much more.

  The initial configuration is almost always done either by the warehouse management system supplier or (preferably) by users with support and assistance from the supplier. Supplier involvement is generally advised because configuration can be complex and a detailed understanding of the system's processes are needed to avoid unintended consequences.

- <u>Loading of dynamic data.</u> Dynamic data in a warehouse management system usually consists of open orders (both inbound and outbound) and current inventory levels within each location. Because this data changes minute-by-minute, it must be loaded after the old system is shut down for the last time and before the new system is started for the

---

[24] Illustration courtesy of Quantronix, Inc. It is presented here as an example and not as an endorsement of Quantronix or its products.

first productive operation[25]. It, therefore, requires detailed coordination with all other startup work.

Many businesses starting warehouse management systems for the first time do not have existing inventory records on a location-by-location basis. Others may have the data, but may not trust it. In either of these cases, a full warehouse physical inventory may be required, an expensive and time-consuming operation. The use of a third-party inventory service may be of value. Unlike product weights and dimensions, it is not recommended that a warehouse management system be taken live with questionable inventory data.

Similarly, order data may require cleansing or at least validation before transfer to the warehouse management system. And similarly, a zero tolerance for errors is advised.

User training

Warehouse management system training is normally required at four levels:

- Warehouse operators, personnel using mobile terminals, and their supervisors require training in the use of these terminals and in the processes and procedures behind them. Operator training should be brief (less than a day) and should be scheduled as late as possible before the go-live day to maximize retention. Other training can be scheduled earlier.

- Warehouse supervisors and managers require training in the general operation of the system and in its general capabilities. This training also extends into available reporting and the system's report generator[26].

- Warehouse engineers (the people responsible for configuration of the system and for warehouse processes and procedures) require detailed training in the system's features and capabilities and in the use of system configuration controls.

- Most warehouse management system suppliers recommend that the user provide first-level IT support with in-house resources and that

---

[25] Dynamic data will actually be required for training and testing purposes as well as at start-up, and therefore it usually must be imported twice. Quality requirements for the initial download of training data, however, are not as high as for the final data.
[26] Some warehouse managers prefer to create their own analyses and reports, while others prefer to use IT resources. Where necessary, management and supervision training should include training in the system's reporting and analytical tools.

supplier support capabilities be used to support the supporters. User IT personnel, therefore, require training in the system's maintenance requirements and in the procedures to be used when supplier support is required[27].

In addition to the training required before go-live, there will be a continuing need for training new personnel and for refresher training for existing operators. The cost of initial training and rights for a company trainer to re-use training materials over time are often included in the software license, but may be priced separately by the supplier.

Business disruption

The costs associated with business disruption during a warehouse management system installation project are frequently overlooked during project planning and justification. Disruption often takes several forms:

> *Time away from regular jobs for project participants*. Not only will project team members risk failing to get needed work done, but the company risks burnout when supervisors and managers attempt to do both their regular jobs and participate in the installation project. The business suffers, both in terms of reduced productivity and worsened customer service and there can even be long-term consequences.

> *Need for an initial inventory and other data collection.* These tasks require both hourly labor and supervision. They are often done on overtime, increasing their cost and reducing the availability of overtime hours for other work. In the extreme, pausing to take a physical inventory can affect customer service and it almost always decreases productivity.

> *Learning curve after go live day.* As we will discuss in the sections on system benefits (starting on page 59), most warehouse management systems are justified based on productivity improvements. Most installations do ultimately achieve improved productivity levels. But there is a hockey-sick effect. As an immediate consequence of the installation, productivity will almost certainly get worse, only later rising to

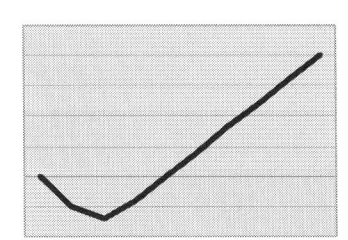

Figure 16. The Hockey Puck curve, showing results over time following project installation

---

[27] If technical support is to be provided entirely in-house by the user, this training becomes extensive.

much improved levels as users come up to speed. This phenomenon is well known and is a consequence of many different kinds of productivity improvement projects. It is primarily caused by the need for users to finish their training and become proficient in the new patterns of work. Generally, consequences of the hockey-stick phenomenon are most significant when management fails to plan for it.

➤ <u>Risk of system imperfections and training inadequacies.</u> As is true with all large customized projects, there is a risk of failing to discover software imperfections and/or training inadequacies before the system is taken live (These two problems often look alike from the viewpoint of the users). Sometimes defects and training issues have quick solutions and are not of major consequence. At other times, however, the solutions may be much harder to find and much more costly to implement. In the extreme, there have been instances in which the warehouse management system was de-installed as a result. The business disruption can be massive.

Contingencies

No major systems project should be justified without admitting that perfect planning is impossible and that, therefore, costs are likely to be higher than anticipated. Some businesses have standards for setting project contingency budgets but, in absence of these standards, this paper suggests that contingency funds be set aside according to the percentages in the table below.

	First time installation with an inexperienced team	Reinstallation in an experienced site
Software licenses	5-10%	3-5%
Hardware	5-10%	3-5%
Integration	15-20%	5-10%
Customization	20-25%	10-15%
All other costs	5-10%	3-5%

Ongoing Operating Costs

Proper evaluation of a warehouse management system requires that both one-time and ongoing or recurring costs be accounted for since only **net** savings justify the one-time costs.

There are some definitional issues in the calculation of ongoing operating costs, since some may be more easily calculated as "negative benefits" in the benefits calculation. For purposes of this paper, ongoing costs are those that are new with the installation of the warehouse management system. Costs that previously existed but are increased as a result of the system installation are handled in the benefits discussion.

There are several sources of ongoing cost.

Software and hardware support

Warehouse management system suppliers typically provide ongoing support for their products at a fee. Unless the user licenses the source code and has the personnel and skills required to take over software support internally, these fees are a necessary part of the project[28].

Some warehouse management system suppliers charge for support on an annual fixed-fee basis, usually charging between 15% and 20% of the initial license fee annually. When custom modifications are made to the software, their support is also fee-based, often as a similar percentage of the amount charged for making the modification. So, for instance, a warehouse management system that licenses for $250,000 and includes $150,000 in modifications might cost between $60,000 and $80,000 per year for support.

System support may also vary with the service required by the user. Most suppliers make around-the-clock service available, but at a premium price. Other suppliers offer guaranteed response times, on-site availability, and/or other services for a premium. Still others may price their services on a per-call, per-transaction, or per-user basis, but the bottom line cost is likely to be similar. Needless to say, support services are a significant profit center for the suppliers.

In recent years, some warehouse management system suppliers have provided global support. A call from the US at 4AM, for instance, might be routed to the

---

[28] Internal support costs should also be determined and included in the system justification since they are not likely to be trivial. Fully burdened costs should be used, of course.

supplier's call center in the UK. This has the advantage that the service is being provided by a technician who is wide awake and ready to begin work immediately, but the obvious disadvantage of distance and relative unfamiliarity with the user's application. (To date, at least, few system suppliers have outsourced their support to third parties.)

In addition to support of the warehouse management system, justification efforts should account for support costs for the computers, RF terminals, RFID equipment, operating system, network, database manager, report generator, and other supporting software.

External support costs, of course, are best estimated by obtaining a supplier quotation. Internal costs are usually best estimated by the people who will be doing the work following detailed discussions with the system supplier.

Supplies

Warehouse management systems typically depend heavily on bar codes and, more recently, on RFID tags (which may be embedded in labels). The cost of label stock, together with the cost of paper, ink and toner for the printers is generally not enough to be a deciding factor in a system justification, but can be enough to be a surprise if no estimate is made. This is especially true for businesses that budget tightly and have no prior experience with warehouse management systems.

Labels, including the costs of printing, can run 25¢ each and if several thousand are used each day, total annual cost can approach $50,000. Costs are still higher for RFID tags embedded in labels.

Configuration and data maintenance

One ongoing cost that has frequently been missed in past warehouse management system project justification studies is the cost of system configuration and data maintenance, needed above and beyond the support and maintenance provided by the system supplier.

For example, most businesses experience a continuing flow of new items or SKUs. Generally each new item must be reviewed at the warehouse level and various parameters must be established for it to control how, where and when it moves. In some businesses it may be possible to automate elements of this work, but in many it will remain a separate and manual operation.

Businesses also see variations in demand for their products over time and these variations require occasional warehouse re-slotting. Even if the warehouse management system includes a fully-automated re-slotting system, someone must be assigned to the management and monitoring of that system and, when an automated re-slotting package is not included, a significant amount of manual work is required to design and implement the necessary changes.

Warehouse expansions, layout changes, personnel and schedule changes, and new or replacement warehouse equipment must also be reflected in the warehouse management system configuration. This work requires a well-trained staff that has time available in the workday to concentrate on issues and bring them to a conclusion. The alternative is gradual loss of the system's productivity gains.

The same people who maintain the system's configuration are often also charged with first-line system support, handling support issues that need not be referred to the supplier. They can often manage problems with system start-up and shut down, advise users on how to manage non-routine tasks such as unloading an outbound trailer that cannot be moved from the dock due to mechanical problems, and handle other semi-technical issues. Some system suppliers will quote lower support prices if the user provides this kind of first-line support.

Estimating the work hours required to maintain a system's configuration and to support changes in the business can be difficult. Experience says that an estimate of approximately 1% to 2% of direct labor costs can be a reasonable starting point. A warehouse employing 100 workers will probably need a full time system manager/engineer, and may need two if it operates a relatively complete second shift. Needless to say, more than one person should be trained for the work to allow vacation and illness coverage and to handle personnel turnover.

Training

Personnel turnover is a fact of life and, therefore, an allowance should be made for the training of new workers, both at the hourly and salaried levels. While this training may be offered by the system supplier, there is also the alternative of providing it in-house, assuming that appropriate people are available. The system supplier may be willing to provide the required training materials and to update them as needed.

Change over time

The estimation of ongoing costs involves a look into the future, which always involves some level of risk and one should be concerned about how these costs can change over time. Without reference to a specific business, estimating change is difficult, but a few points can be made:

- Labor-related costs (primarily support) will tend to decline as users gain knowledge of the system and experience using it.

- The cost of supplies (labels, etc.) will naturally change with changed warehouse volume

- Configuration maintenance costs will relate to the frequency of change to processes and procedures in the warehouse as well as to changes in product volume and mix

- Training costs will vary with warehouse turnover

Benefits

The great majority of warehouse management system installations made in past years have been justified based on productivity improvement in the warehouse, but simple cost reduction is not the only benefit available. Warehouse management systems, under the right circumstances and in the right businesses, can also provide major boosts in customer service and can achieve things that are nearly impossible in a manual, paper-driven environment. For example, regulatory requirements in some businesses can make a warehouse management system mandatory, regardless of any cost savings.

This discussion divides the benefits of a warehouse management system into quantitative (measurable) and qualitative (non-measurable) groups. The following discussion on ROI calculation (see page 69) describes how these two groups can be combined into a single financial picture of the proposed project.

A word about supplier estimates: Most warehouse management system suppliers will be happy to help estimate the benefits available from an installation of their software and some will even provide extensive operations analyses to support their claims. This paper advises that supplier estimates be carefully reviewed and given detailed consideration. The suppliers, of course, have a great deal of experience with their systems and with the results achieved. However, it almost goes without saying that the supplier's motivation is to sell its software and that there is motivation to exaggerate. We do not, therefore, recommend that supplier estimates be used without detailed confirmation. They may be best taken as a source of ideas for an internally created justification analysis.

Quantitative benefits

The quantitative benefits available from a warehouse management system fall almost entirely into the area of labor cost reduction, also called productivity improvement. Depending on one's viewpoint, these systems tend to make the operators' jobs easier, allowing them to achieve more with the same level of effort, or reduce unnecessary steps, allowing more to be done in a day with a given workforce, or simply allow management to reduce the size of the workforce or get more work done with the existing staff.

The first, and usually the most important source of productivity improvement comes from making material handlers more efficient. These improvements generally apply across the warehouse including the receiving, putaway, picking, replenishing, packing and shipping functions. Examples of common improvements include:

- Optimum organization of work reduces travel time in the warehouse and, where interleaving is in use, reduces unloaded travel.

- Rational work planning eliminates unnecessary work and focuses operators on only the work required to get the job done

- Development of work plans based on real-time, accurate inventory records eliminates operator travel to locations that do not contain the needed product and eliminates the need for operators to search for product.

- Order consolidations eliminate many unnecessary picks when customers place multiple orders in a single day.

- Automated support for (and enforcement of) specialized picking methods such as batch picking, bulk picking, pick-and-pass, and others. These methods are used when they, in turn, reduce cost.

- Automated use of ASNs reduces or mostly eliminates the need to sort, identify and count arriving material.

- Cross-docking techniques eliminate separate put-away, replenishment and picking activities. Similarly, direct putaway to forward picking eliminates replenishment work.

- System-directed putaway eliminates the need for operators to search for an appropriate putaway location and also significantly supports management's desired physical organization/layout.

- System-defined and directed pick location replenishment allows replenishment moves to be better timed and larger. This, in turn, reduces both pick shortages and replenishment labor.

- Cartonization, when used in the right situation, can eliminate the need for a separate packing operation.

- Automated (or semi-automated) returns handling processes speed product identification, evaluation and sortation and assist with the credit issuing process.

- Validation of all movements ensures accuracy, supporting improved work planning and reducing errors. Error reduction, in turn, reduces the effort required to correct errors and increases customer satisfaction.

- RF dispatching of work eliminates much handling of paper and eliminates the time required for operators to travel to a central location to pick up paper at the start of each assignment. It effectively allows continuous work.

- Picking validation processes often eliminate the need for a separate order checking function and thus eliminate the staff required.

- Monitoring of operator productivity in real time allows management to quickly identify and act on personnel and training issues as they arise.

- Visibility into near-term future workloads gives management the ability to better plan staffing, minimize overtime and maximize customer service.

- Direct, real-time interfaces with material handling equipment makes sophisticated automation possible and integrates it into the rest of the operation.

- Yard management functions perform similar tasks in the trailer yard and eliminate or reduce waiting time in shipping and receiving between loads

Additional productivity improvement often comes from a reduction in clerical and supervisory work. In some instances these improvements can be as important as or even more important than material handling productivity improvements. Examples include:

- Elimination of the need to prepare paper pick lists and packing lists. Elimination of other manually prepared shipping paper including manifests, bills of lading, shipping labels, export documentation and more.

- Elimination of data entry and recordkeeping relating to orders (both receipts and shipments) and work completed. Includes the elimination of duplicate data entry in multiple systems.

- Manual dispatching of work to material handlers is no longer required since the system does it automatically

- Online, real-time order status allows fast response to customer, supplier and management queries. Some systems even provide direct web access to order status for authorized customers and suppliers.

- Automated appointments and yard movements reduce manual processes related to inbound and outbound trailers.

> Hourly workforce record keeping is automated as a byproduct of RF processes, making disciplinary actions more effective with little or no clerical work.

The third important source of productivity improvement comes from increased inventory and record accuracy: elimination of the periodic (annual) mass physical inventory in which everything in the warehouse is counted at the same time.

It is a well-documented fact that mass physical inventory taking tends to reduce the accuracy of inventory records in all but the sloppiest warehouses. Counting is boring work with few rewards for accuracy and many for speed, particularly as the day proceeds and the pressures to get done and get the warehouse back to work begin to mount.

Auditors (or less often, regulators) almost always drive the practice of taking mass physical inventories. They are interested entirely in record accuracy and, almost always, when they can be shown that the inventories are accurate before the inventory is taken, their demands will tend to melt away. However, it may be a year or two after the installation of a warehouse management system before accuracy levels are sufficient and during this time, physical inventories may continue to be necessary.

A warehouse management system, coupled with a good program of cycle counting (which is supported by essentially all warehouse management systems) can eliminate the mass periodic physical inventory. This, in turn:

> Saves the labor cost of the physical inventory

> Eliminates the cost of preparing for the inventory including both management work and the cost of training the workforce.

> Allows the business to operate continuously by eliminating the need to shut down for the physical inventory or – for companies that do the inventory on weekends – eliminates the overtime needed.

Warehouse management systems can also provide a number of quantifiable benefits that are not labor related.

> Reduced damage and losses. Because warehouse management systems are structured to minimize material handling costs, they also often reduce the number of times the product is touched. This, in turn, tends to reduce product damage in the warehouse. Further, easy identification and documentation of damage found in receiving reduces the amount not reported to carriers and tends to increase the amount collected on

freight claims. And traceability through system history tables allows management to identify workers who frequently damage material.

- Reduced obsolescence and product expiration losses. System enforced stock rotation (as specified by management in the system configuration) reduces obsolescence and product expiration losses by assuring that the oldest product is shipped first.

- Inventory reduction. Increased inventory record accuracy reduces the need for the business to carry safety stock and thus reduces overall inventory levels. This, in turn, increases space availability in the warehouse, reduces inventory financing and carrying costs and often reduces insurance costs. Note that inventory reductions also provide a one-time cash flow benefit.

- Support for existing software. The warehouse management system can also eliminate support costs for software being taken out of service.

- Warehouse management systems improve warehouse space utilization, primarily by intelligently loading shelves and racks to capacity according to management's rules and directions. Reduced need for inventory also decreases the need for space, as does rational stock rotation.

  Space utilization is further enhanced by allowing inventory to be logically classified and by eliminating much need to physically segregate inventory by, for instance, its quality. Whenever physical separation of inventories is required, additional space is needed, so the collapsing of these requirements reduces the need for space.

  The value of space utilization is most easily evaluated when leased space can be vacated, buildings closed, or a future need for additional space avoided.

- The ability of a warehouse management system to track countries of origin, duty status, material hazards, product serial numbers, expiration dates, and similar attributes is sometimes necessary to meet regulatory requirements. The system automates this tracking, and significantly reduces fines and penalties. In addition, management may choose to assign a higher value based on corporate citizenship and moral values.

Estimating Quantitative Benefits

Having a neat list of the benefits available from a warehouse management system is a good starting point, but the objective is to calculate the project's expected return on investment (ROI), a single number that will yield a clean go/no-go decision. Evaluating benefits in the context of a specific business and a specific situation is rarely easy. This paper suggests three methods: simulation, engineering analysis, and experience-driven estimation.

Simulation

One dictionary defines the verb "to simulate" as "to assume the appearance a thing, without the reality of it." A computer simulation, therefore, is a computer program that assumes the appearance of a thing or a process without the necessity for it to actually exist.

In other words, simulation is the modeling of a physical process in software and data.

Figure 17. View of a warehouse simulation

The purpose of a simulation is typically to allow measurement of complex relationships between process factors for the purpose of predicting process results based on a defined set of inputs. A simulation, therefore, can model the operation of a warehouse using either current or projected systems, procedures and equipment. Measured simulation results parallel the real world, and thus can be used to draw conclusions about proposed changes.

Simulation is probably the most accurate way to estimate warehouse management benefits. However, it can be an expensive and time-consuming exercise in itself. Simulation requires specialized software tools and people with skills that may be hard to find. Further, the degree to which senior managers will accept the outcome of a warehouse simulation depends on the sophistication of the managers themselves. Some simply fail to understand.

A few consultants have simulation skills and have tools available that can dramatically reduce the cost of building a warehouse simulation. In the right circumstances, simulation can be both reasonably priced and reasonably fast.

Engineering analysis

Engineering analysis can be difficult to describe because it involves a degree of ad-hoc creativity. It amounts, however, to the collection of operating information and the analysis of that information in numbers to determine benefit levels.

For example, imagine a proposed warehouse management system installation that will allow the batch picking of orders for the first time. The engineer[29] could draw a sample of orders and could calculate the time required to pick those orders based on product locations (which allows estimation of travel distance and thus travel time) and pick time. The orders could then be formed into batches and the analysis repeated for the batches. While the work can be painstaking, it can also be revealing. If enough analysis is done, benefits can be accurately determined.

The engineer, however, needs to be careful that benefits are not double-counted. For instance, the savings associated with batch picking may duplicate savings associated with providing RF terminals to the operators.

Experience-Driven Estimation

The fastest and easiest way to estimate warehouse management system benefits is by comparison with other known installations of the same (or a similar) warehouse management system. People who have worked in other sites with similar systems, and especially people who have experienced warehouse management system installation projects, may have knowledge of the benefits actually gained and may be able to adjust those benefits to fit the current situation.

While the analysis required for experience-driven estimation can be mathematically simple, there is significant reliance on judgment and the results are generally less reliable than other methods. Consultants with broad experience (and no axe to grind) are often the best source of these types of estimates.

There is, of course, a temptation to use vendor-supplied estimates. While system vendors have the required breadth and depth of experience, their biases are obvious and should be carefully considered before accepting their estimates of the savings to be made.

---

[29] Use of the term "engineer" should not be taken to mean that a degreed engineer is required. The term "analyst" could be used equally well.

Qualitative benefits

Warehouse management systems offer many different savings and benefits, some of which are very hard to quantify. These qualitative benefits, however, can be important and in some instances, can be more important than the quantitative ones. They should not be ignored.

Benefits that cannot be numerically estimated can only be described. However, some of those discussed in this section may be quantifiable in some businesses. If numeric estimation of the value of any of these items is possible, it should be done in preference to a qualitative statement.

A method for combining qualitative and quantitative benefits into a single value statement for the warehouse management system project appears in the section "Calculating ROI," found on page 69.

Customer Service

The single most important qualitative benefit is customer service. Improved customer service, of course, translates into increased sales that result in increased profitability. The problem is that the determination of how many additional sales will result from a change in service levels is very difficult.

Warehouse management systems may improve customer service by:

> Getting product into customers' hands faster and enabling more reliable and more repeatable lead times.

  Speed through the logistics process is achieved, first, by automating paperwork and eliminating delay, second, by concentrating workers' effort on the work that really needs to be done (by assuring that priorities are observed), and third, by eliminating much lost and wasted time.

  Yard management systems track inbound trailer content, allowing hot items to be moved to the docks faster and, in total, moving product to customers faster.

> Improving accuracy throughout the supply chain

  Increasing accuracy in receiving, picking, shipping and all material handling activities makes it possible for delivery promises to be more accurate (because stock levels are known with certainty) and reduces mis-picks and both wrong-item and wrong-quantity shipments. Increased accuracy reduces complaints, follow-up effort, and returns.

> Providing better and more reliable compliance with customer requirements

  Strict and reliable adherence to customer (and carrier) requirements reduces chargebacks (a quantifiable savings), but also reduces receiving hassle for the customer and enhances customer satisfaction. Many of these requirements involve value-added[30] services.

> Enforced stock rotation improves freshness

  Complex customer freshness requirements can be met automatically and with minimum management attention. Better control reduces customer dissatisfaction and eliminates many returns, while also reducing any legal liabilities that may be involved.

> Better control over product quality issues including damage

  Control over obsolete, damaged, past-date, and defective product and its shipment increases customer satisfaction and may reduce liabilities.

Accuracy

The increased accuracy provided by warehouse management systems has benefit beyond customer satisfaction. Accuracy enhances management's ability to plan, helps reduce inventory levels, and can actually increase employee satisfaction by reducing frustration.

Warehouse management systems provide accuracy primarily by validating material movements. They also support cycle counting and usually allow physical inventories to be eliminated. They provide unit of measure conversions and store data that allows operators to be held accountable for their work.

Product Quality Management

Product quality management includes the ability to track inventories by product grade (firsts, seconds, etc.), the ability to identify and track damage, product aging facilities, and support for a variety of product holds. Sometimes this tracking replaces fallible manual processes and other times it provides entirely new capabilities. Most warehouse management systems can be interfaced to quality management systems for still more extensive capabilities.

Quality management increases customer satisfaction (as noted above), limits exposure to legal liabilities, and enhances the company's image and brand.

---

[30] Value-added services are defined and discussed starting on page 20.

Ownership Tracking

The ability to track product ownership pallet-by-pallet, carton-by-carton, or even piece-by-piece is critical in the 3PL industry, where the warehousing company does not own the product stored and where product from several owners may be stored in a single facility. It can also have significant value in other installations.

Ownership tracking can make possible the management of consigned goods and can allow normal warehouses to accept and manage third-party goods, sometimes allowing excess space to be used profitably. It is also very useful when suppliers help finance inventories through delayed billing (which necessarily involves mixed product ownership).

Employee turnover

When a high-quality warehouse management system is properly installed and when the workers are well trained and highly motivated, they will find themselves actually exerting less effort and working under less stress. The operators actually enjoy working with these systems and their pleasure is reflected in reduced turnover and training.

Employee Safety

Safety in a warehousing environment is largely a matter of training, providing and properly maintaining the right equipment, and maintaining proper discipline. Warehouse management systems, however, contribute by:

- Assuring that equipment (both storage and material handling) is not overloaded

- Limiting workers to appropriate tasks based on the equipment they are using and their level of training.

Management Control

And finally, warehouse management systems offer the potential for unprecedented levels of management information and control.

Warehouse management systems maintain very large and detailed real-time databases and extensive history files. This data can be a gold mine of management information for the warehouse manager and for other senior management. Analytical and reporting tools, in imaginative and capable hands, are able to produce a dizzying variety of previously unavailable information. Progress and status of orders, waves, inventories, operators, vehicles, and space can be tracked and monitored in real time. And event management functions including configurable alarms and alerts can guarantee immediate knowledge of issues and thus can enable significantly faster and more accurate response.

Calculating ROI

The object of all the planning, specifying and estimating done is project justification. Will, in fact, the project be worth doing? Should work proceed?

Justification can be financial or non-financial. In most businesses, projects are easiest to sell if the justification is financial, so we begin with calculations to determine either a Return on Investment (ROI) or a Payback Period. Most companies have established thresholds for one or the other of these two measures (or for both) and if the project meets that threshold, justification is simple.

Some warehouse management systems, however, are not financially justifiable, but are still necessary to the business. Justification for these projects, therefore, is based on non-quantifiable issues and the approach to management for project approval must be based on the financial cost of resolving those issues.

Appendix B (page 133) contains a worksheet that outlines the calculations required in detail. This worksheet is intended to assist project managers and engineers in the evaluation of proposed warehouse management projects. It lists evaluations that may need to be done and quotations that may need to be obtained, provides a place to record them, and leads the user through the process of calculating the return on investment and payback period for the proposed project.

WMS Weaknesses

While this paper has concentrated on the costs and benefits associated with a warehouse management system, they aren't the whole story. There are two more items that should be discussed here because either the software suppliers and many current users won't admit to them, or because they won't think to mention them.

Possibly the biggest potential downside of a warehouse management system is the fact that, once installed, the business becomes wholly dependent on it. If the computer goes down, the warehouse is down. With appropriate precautions, this is a minor concern, but it must be recognized and planned for.

Paper-based backup systems have been tried, but are generally not worthwhile. Once a system is past the initial growing pains, the lost productivity caused by downtime is almost always less than the cost of keeping a parallel paper system running. Instead, the best solutions are:

- Quality software
- Thorough training
- Detailed testing before go-live (discussed in more detail later)
- Redundant (or partially redundant) hardware
- Fast and reliable support

The most important of these factors are probably training and testing. Testing is especially important when installing custom modified software since the modifications do not have the benefit of experience in other businesses. Training (or the lack of it) and a consequent failure to understand how the system is supposed to work, probably causes more system problems than any other single factor. Go-live testing should test not only the software, but also the people who will use it.

The other important, but largely un-discussed factor is that the warehouse management system changes the business in fundamental ways. Disciple is required of the users to a degree never before needed. Not only must the users understand how the system works and how it should be used, they must also actually do what the system instructs them to do. And when the system's instructions make less than perfect sense, the only reasonable solution is to fix the system, not to ignore it.

Work done without keeping the system up to date must absolutely cease. Knowledgeable system engineers must investigate needed workarounds in detail before they are put into practice. And everyone must understand that, in a very real sense, the system is running the warehouse.

Organizational Impact

The installation of a warehouse management system changes the demands placed on the warehouse's management organization and thus may require organizational change. In a broad sense, the "bull of the woods" who rose through the ranks and could run the warehouse based on scraps of paper is no longer the ideal person. The new challenge is more technical and more detailed.

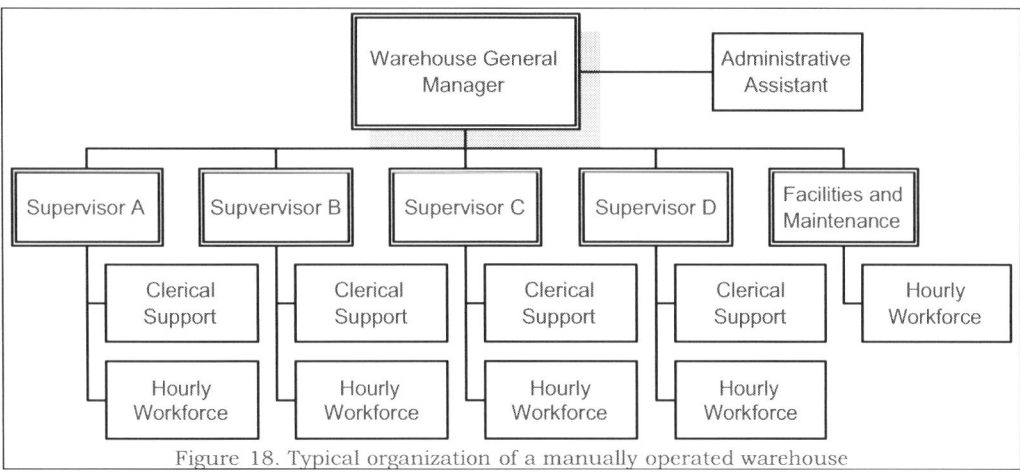
Figure 18. Typical organization of a manually operated warehouse

Figure 18 illustrates the organization of a typical large warehouse prior to the installation of a warehouse management system. Figure 19 illustrates the same warehouse, re-organized to accommodate the system.

The organization change shown in Figure 19 is mostly a matter of emphasis. The number of clerical workers employed has decreased (possibly to zero), so the remaining work has been centralized. Offsetting this gain is the addition of a "warehouse engineering" staff.

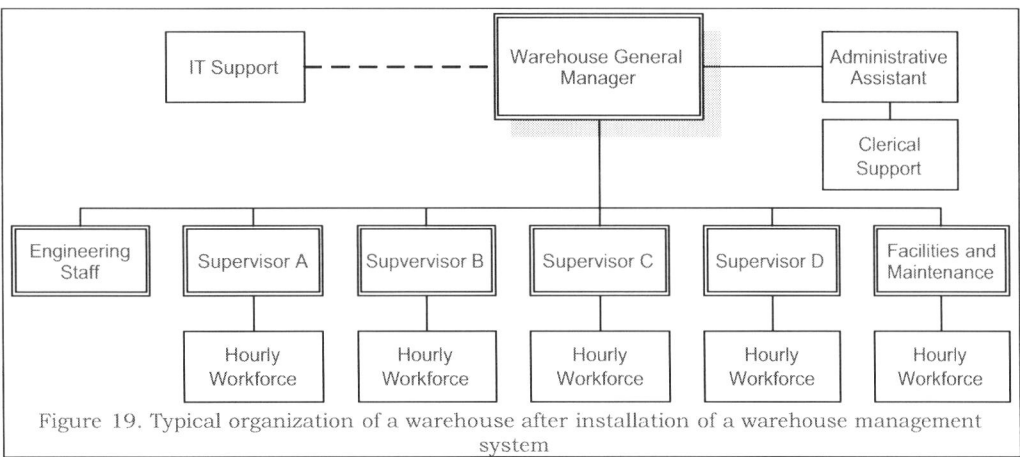
Figure 19. Typical organization of a warehouse after installation of a warehouse management system

The warehouse engineer(s) need not be degreed nor do they need advanced skills. They are the people who are responsible for managing and maintaining the system's configuration and for certain elements of system data. Job qualifications include a numeric aptitude, creativity, an understanding of management's short and long term goals, and attention to detail.

The warehouse engineer's primary job often includes:

- Maintenance of the warehouse system configuration as processes, product, equipment and people change
- Investigations into and implementation of process improvements
- Management of the flow of new items
- Planning of changes to warehouse structure and equipment and reflection of these changes in the system configuration
- Playing a role in training new warehouse workers

The idea of a "staff" need not imply a large number of people. Simple warehouses with easy-to-handle products require only one part time engineer. The very largest and most complex may require two or possibly three full time people. The important thing is that someone has these responsibilities and the time to get the work done.

The warehouse management system will require in-house IT support although, depending on the support received from the software supplier, the amount needed may be small. Most warehouses provide this support from an existing IT organization through a dotted line relationship, but large organizations with large warehouses sometimes employ IT professionals directly in the logistics organization.

And finally, the organization should recognize that the installation of a warehouse management system is likely to require learning a new set of terminology. Terms like zone, wave and location have very specific meanings in most warehouse management systems and failure to understand the implications of these terms can create unnecessary confusion and even conflict. While new terminology is hardly a critical problem, it is best if the organization recognizes and accepts the need for change.

Who Should Have a WMS?

Simply put, organizations that can justify a warehouse management system should have one. Either the return on investment should meet company requirements or the system's non-quantifiable benefits should justify their cost in management's judgment.

But at a higher level, there are several characteristics that tend strongly to predict success of failure in a system justification effort. These characteristics may help determine whether or not a system justification study should even be performed[31]. Included are:

- Discrete products. Warehouse management systems easily handle raw materials, work in progress and finished goods, but only for discrete products. If a significant percentage of your product is handled in bulk and moved through pipes by pumps or blowers, then a warehouse management system is unlikely to have great value.

- Break bulk. Warehouses that simply receive and ship units and do not break bulk will have more difficulty justifying a warehouse management system, mostly because of the simplicity and low labor content of their operations. Examples include pure freight transfer operations and some beverage warehouses.

- Warehouse size and complexity. The smallest and simplest warehouses are unlikely to be able to justify a warehouse management system. As a general rule of thumb, a warehouse with simple products that employs less than a dozen full time material handlers is unlikely to find justification. (Note that warehouse physical size is almost irrelevant. It is activity that creates justification.) Small warehouses with very complex products or those that are heavily regulated by government may still find justification but below three or four material handlers the chances drop off dramatically.

- Wage rates. In some countries, prevailing wage rates are so low that justification through labor savings becomes impossible. This is almost never a problem in any of the developed nations.

---

[31] These characteristics do not necessarily rule out the profitable use of a computer. The optimum software, however, probably would not fit our definition of a warehouse management system but might be better characterized as an inventory locator system.

The WMS Project

This executive briefing is not intended to be a primer in general software project management and therefore it discusses only tissues unique to warehouse management system projects. For general software project management, we suggest:

- *Software Project Management: A Unified Framework* by Walker Royce (Addison-Wesley, 1998)
- *Applied Software Project Management* by Andrew Stellman and Jennifer Greene (O'Reilly Media, 2005)
- *Software Project Management in Practice* by Pankai Jalote (Addison-Wesley, 2002)
- *Buying Software: A Best Practice Approach* (Stationery Office Books, 2004)

With that said, it is a fact that warehouse management system selection and installation projects differ little from the projects required for any major software system. The material below discusses a few considerations that senior management should understand before the project is launched. Following sections discuss the unique aspects of the market for warehouse management systems and go into more detail on the various phases of the software project. The final section of this briefing discusses special operational considerations.

First Time vs. Reinstallation

There is a significant difference between a first-time warehouse management project and a reinstallation or system replacement project. The difference, of course, lies primarily in organizational knowledge and experience. The gap between a paper-driven warehouse and a system-driven one is much larger than the gap between different versions of a warehouse management system or even different warehouse management systems from different suppliers.

Make vs. Buy

How many firms do you know that have written and support their own word processing software? Similarly, the advantages of a licensed warehouse management system almost always far outweigh the disadvantages of having to deal with a third party.

> Warehouse management system suppliers do not release investment information, but it is a fair guess that the tier one suppliers have each spent at least $25 million on product development and testing. It is hard to imagine that even a very basic system could be written from scratch for less than $5 million. License purchases, however, together with all required services rarely run over $1 million, even for the largest facilities.

> The purchase of a software license gives the user access to software than has, for the most part, been thoroughly tested in dozens or possibly hundreds of businesses.

> Commercial warehouse management systems now have many best practices built into them. Internally developed systems often miss these best practices and tend to perpetuate existing less than optimum ways of doing business.

> Support for commercial systems is provided by people who do nothing else on a full time basis. They tend, therefore, to be faster, more accurate, and more efficient than is possible for an internal staff that supports a variety of software.

However, the advantage that commercial warehouse management systems have over internally developed systems has not always existed. Some businesses developed their own warehouse management system in the 1980s and 1990s. With the initial development cost now written off, these firms may well find continued support and occasional enhancement more effective than the purchase of a commercial license.

In general, the reader who is considering a warehouse management system where none now exists should be leery of proposals for internal development. However, the reader who is currently supporting an internally developed system should carefully consider the issue of make vs. buy.

Timeline Expectations

Some firms have entered into warehouse management system projects with unrealistic expectations. Since most businesses have some degree of seasonality, and since there is significant benefit to doing a warehouse management system installation during the quiet season, a good understanding of the likely size and duration of the project has value.

The total elapsed time for a warehouse management system project varies significantly with

- The size and complexity of the operation
- Internal resources dedicated to the project.

The simplest and smallest warehouses can usually be implemented and running four to six months from project launch, but this assumes that project team members are provided with adequate resources and that the project is their top priority. If the team also has day-to-day operations responsibilities and can only work on the project in their spare time, and if any allowance is to be made for error, then a nine to twelve month schedule may be more appropriate.

Larger warehouses with more complex operations require more extensive projects and thus these projects take more time. Again measuring from project launch, a year to eighteen months is quite normal. And if there are unique requirements that demand major software modification by the supplier, or if host systems require significant modification, the timeline can extend beyond eighteen months.

These timelines can be compressed by providing the project team with additional resources and by setting deadlines, but it's generally best not to press too hard. Shortcuts and unwarranted assumptions generally result in less than optimum results.

One generally need not be concerned about software and hardware suppliers dragging their heels. They, of course, are paid when the project is complete. Exceptions occur only when the software supplier has more work than he or she can handle.

Achieving Success

According to a study sponsored by *Supply Chain Technology News* several years ago, over half of all WMS installations have failed to deliver value at anticipated levels. The top reasons cited for failure were:

➤ Project Creep

A warehouse management system installation project is almost always a learning process for the project team. As time passes and work is completed, ideas pop up and it can be hard to resist the thought that a little change here and a tiny one there would have benefit. This is called project creep – the continued accumulation of small changes through the life of the project. Often, when the project is complete, the total change is found to be substantial, even though no individual change amounted to much.

Project creep is not a bad thing. The small changes identified during the project can have value out of proportion to their cost. The management challenge, however, is to maintain control over the project so that creep does not unduly delay implementation or unreasonably increase cost.

The best policy is probably to encourage ideas, but to require that team members (and system suppliers) use a formal change control process with appropriate cost justification and approvals.

➤ Failure to Identify Expectations From the Start

Some firms consider their business practices and their warehouse management system justification analyses to be confidential and are reluctant to share them with the software supplier. Assuming that the supplier has signed an appropriate non-disclosure agreement, this is poor policy. The supplier, of course, cannot work to achieve goals that he or she does not know exist.

➤ Transition Between Sales and Implementation Teams

Almost all warehouse management system suppliers have separate sales and implementation organizations. Therefore, the smiling and congenial sales rep that takes you to lunch before the contract is signed is likely to disappear before the ink is dry. In some projects in the past, this has caused problems.

You have no control over the supplier's organization, but can insist on a smooth transition between the sales and implementation teams. Following contract signature, there should be a project kick-off meeting, attended by the supplier's sales rep, its installation project manager, and key members of its installation project team. You, as senior manager, together with your project manager and key members of your project team should also attend. The supplier's senior management should be invited, but the meeting should not bc dclaycd if they are unable to attend.

See page 114 for more information on the kick-off meeting.

➢ Executive Support

Although the user's executives will not likely play a day-to-day role in the system selection and installation project, their support is critical. Support, in this instance, implies two things: First, changes made to the top-level goals and objectives will be disruptive and inefficient and should be made only after considering the consequences. And second, the project team will need reliable resources to achieve the desired timeline. Senior management should make early commitments to supply the needed resources and then should recognize that any changes made to those commitments will have consequences beyond the team's control

➢ Modifications

Software modifications are not necessarily either a good or a bad thing. However, excessive, unnecessary or poorly specified modification can result in project failure.

Management should examine each modification. First, each should be justifiable on its own. Each modification, that is to say, should increase the ROI of the total project and should not decrease it. And second, there should also be positive ROI for inclusion of the modification in the initial installation project, as opposed to deferring it to a later upgrade project. Some modifications, of course, will be much more expensive if deferred. Others can be deferred at little cost and if the benefits impact is acceptable, should be deferred to keep the initial project as simple and manageable as possible.

➢ KISS

There can be great temptation to combine the warehouse management system project with other project work such as warehouse layout changes, other system installations, management structure changes, new facilities, and more. In some instances, there can be good reason to do so, but in general, the KISS principle (Keep It Simple, Stupid), rules. The process of selecting, licensing and installing a warehouse management system is complex enough in itself. Wherever possible, other projects should be done separately.

➢ Inadequate Training

Warehouse management systems require user and technical training at several levels. Some installation projects have failed in the past because the training was either inadequate, or was presented to the users too early.

Team members will require early and detailed training. On-the-floor users, however, should be given only the training they need to continue doing the work they are responsible for and that training should be provided at the latest possible time so it isn't forgotten.

This paper strongly recommends an exercise called a "mock go-live" which, among other things, reinforces the training given to the hourly workforce and which can be very important in a smooth startup. See "The Installation Project" starting on page 113 for more details.

The user's primary defense against these issues is its project team. Therefore, the selection of team members and their motivation and management are all critical factors.

Project Staff Turnover

Ultimately, of course, you cannot control turnover in your own organization, in the supplier's organization, or on the project team. Even so, you should be aware that turnover can cause big problems and should be avoided wherever possible. Most software suppliers and most experienced project managers strongly associate the words "reorganization" and "replacement" with the word "catastrophe".

> A large manufacturing company paid a software supplier nearly $100,000 for a detailed system survey and design study. The completed study proposed about $1,000,000 worth of hardware and software; the user projected a 9-month payback. Contract negotiations were nearing completion when the VP of Operations was promoted. No one else in upper management was willing to sign the contract at the time because no one else was familiar with the project and with its projected costs and benefits. Later, the new VP of Operations had other priorities. Net result: the company spent a pile of money and got nothing for it.

User-Supplier Relations

This writer has spent thirty years in the commercial software industry in capacities ranging from programming to project and product management, sales, and business management and has participated in at least twenty major system implementations. Some installations have been spectacular successes; others have been dismal failures. Reflection over the years gives us the ability, within a reasonable margin of error, to predict relative success on many jobs, even before the contract is signed.

It is, of course, true that neither the user nor the supplier is uniformly at fault when installation projects fail or are unduly difficult or expensive. As a software supplier, we certainly haven't been blameless. It is also true that our natural biases at least partially blind us to supplier-related factors that contribute to failure. However, there are also user-related factors, which we see more clearly.

When systems are sold turnkey (i.e., with the supplier accepting responsibility for integration and installation), the single most important factor on the user's side of the fence is the establishment and maintenance of an excellent working relationship with the supplier. Collaboration, in other words, is critical.

Devil is in the Details

Customers who are willing to get involved in the details usually succeed; those who aren't almost always fail.

> One recent installation involved a customer who was quite concerned about the human-engineering aspects of the system. His staff put a great deal of time into review of the supplier's design, made many valuable and detailed comments, and even redesigned some of the physical aspects of the workstations where shop floor data collection terminals were to be used. Despite some hardware-related problems, this system is in place and operating smoothly. The customer is happy because he is getting the benefits he expected from the system. Much of the credit goes to his willingness to take part in the project and get involved in details.

Organizations that purchase major systems can't afford to ignore details, particularly in the area of real-world interfaces and human engineering. Even "turn-key" suppliers contract only to handle system internals and to meet external interface specifications. Not only does your supplier know much less than you do about how your business and your people work on a day-to-day basis, he or she probably doesn't care.

Staff your systems installation projects with people who know how to read and study and who do a lot of reading and studying. Avoid people with superficial knowledge and no propensity for doing their homework.

Trust, But Not Too Much

Customers who place undue amounts of trust in suppliers don't necessarily fail, but they often have a lot tougher time attaining even marginal success.

> A Cleveland manufacturing company installed a system with a custom payroll calculation a number of years ago. At the last minute, the customer's president accelerated our installation schedule, directing that we eliminate parallel testing. He had faith that we would make it work.
>
> The result was disaster. Major flaws came to light after the point of no return had been reached and we found ourselves explaining to union leadership why the payroll was late. The bugs were eventually fixed and the system was eventually successful, but we all came out of the project a lot wiser than we went in.

Select suppliers you can trust to do the job right, but don't bet the farm on them.

Estimates vs. Quotes

Pay attention when your supplier says he is estimating. Price estimates are only estimates and the assumption that they are anything else is foolhardy.

Suppliers are often asked to "ballpark" a project and then find themselves trying to account for the cost difference between the "ballpark" and a firm quotation that was developed later after the user decided on detailed specifications.

Almost all customized software suppliers price their projects based on cost. When you ask for a price, the supplier doesn't simply lift a price out of a book; substantial work is involved. A full-blown system quotation could easily cost between $20,000 and $50,000 to produce. Few suppliers will spend resources at that level to produce a ballpark price. Most will simply rely on experience and judgment. Recognize that ballparks are ballparks, and estimates are estimates. Don't rely on them too heavily.

Validate Specifications

When you buy systems, expect to get what you ask for, and little more.

> Recently one supplier received a Request for Quotation from an apparel manufacturer. The RFQ was poorly written, unclear, and filled with typos. After several long telephone conversations, the supplier felt that he understood the company's requirements well enough to prepare a quotation and ultimately quoted about $450,000 for the project. That firm quickly became the preferred supplier and just as quickly lost the project when a new interpretation of the specifications brought to light more requirements, which forced a price increase.
>
> Although the supplier was disappointed at the loss of the job, the real damage was done to the customer by its project manager. In effect, he forced his company to choose its software supplier based on flawed and probably erroneous information.

System specifications are the key. Read you own specifications both before sending them out and before contracting with a system supplier. Ruthlessly eliminate wording that might be misunderstood – particularly your own internal company terminology. Be sure that your specifications include everything that is important to you, and nothing that isn't important. Then, later, if you find something that you need that wasn't specified, expect the supplier to charge for adding it.

Commercially Available Systems

Only a fool would make a major purchase in the stock market without understanding at least the basics of how the market works and what it offers. Similarly, before embarking on a warehouse management system project, it is a good idea to learn a little about the market for such systems.

Brief Industry History

Warehouse management systems were first developed as inventory control systems, mostly by users' internal staff as an outgrowth of then-new manufacturing shop floor control systems. Operating almost entirely in batch mode, these systems were first implemented in the middle 1970s and began to attract some attention before the end of the decade. A small group of privately held companies saw potential in the idea and by 1980 there were probably a half-dozen firms – none larger than 25 or 30 employees – who were effectively promoting and selling warehouse management systems.

Early warehouse management systems used offline portable data collection terminals that were carried by workers and returned to a central point several times a day to upload completed work into the system. Data, therefore, was not maintained in real time. The concept of radio terminals (RF terminals) soon was integrated into these systems and, by about 1985, almost all warehouse management systems featured a choice of RF or batch terminals. Before the end of the 1980s, the use of batch terminals had essentially ceased in recognition of the value of real-time data.

The UNIX operating system had originated in 1969, but was owned and controlled by AT&T for many years. It wasn't until IBM introduced its AIX version and Hewlett Packard its HP-UX version, that UNIX became commercially viable. These introductions coincided with huge growth in the warehouse management system market. Most systems, to this date, had been written for whatever platform the customer wanted, but the 1990s saw more and more suppliers abandon their traditional platforms in favor of the newly popular UNIX. Some were able to adapt existing code, while others chose a complete re-write.

Increased volume in the industry attracted new firms, many of which struggled to survive in competition with the older and more established ones. By 1998, several major suppliers had issued IPOs and a few of them are still publicly held. The tech meltdown of 2000, however brought an end to IPOs and today, with a few exceptions, most of the industry is privately held.

Early warehouse systems included only basic function and almost always required customization, but suppliers quickly identified needed improvements and took advantage of opportunities to convert user-financed customizations into new system features. By the middle 1990s, improved standard system function started a no-modification trend in warehouse management system installations. Increasing system functionality has now reached the point where custom modification is far less common and usually much less complex than it once was.

Also through the 1990s, the market for warehouse management systems changed. When the industry began, almost all installations were made in warehouses that had never before had such a system. By 2000, however, market saturation began to be felt and, today, the great majority of system licensing deals are done to replace one warehouse management system with another. Market saturation has affected the way warehouse management systems are sold and has changed the business model for many suppliers.

Major Product Options

Warehouse management system offerings in today's market can be characterized in several ways. These differences should be understood before starting a warehouse management system project since they can provide a reasonable an inexpensive way for companies to make preliminary system selection decisions

Platforms

With a few exceptions, warehouse management systems today are offered for one of three platforms. The choice of platform is usually important because the incremental support cost of introducing a new platform into a business can be significant.

- Unix. The most common platform in warehouse management systems is Unix. These systems tend to be relatively mature and relatively complete.
- AS/400. There are still a few systems offered for the AS/400 platform and they can represent real value for existing AS/400 users. There is, however, little new development work being done for the AS/400 and no systems are being ported to it.
- Microsoft. The most common platform for smaller systems is the Microsoft technology "stack." Originally the home of smaller systems intended for smaller warehouses, increased throughput capabilities and

decreased support costs have encouraged many top-tier warehouse management system suppliers to convert their code to the Microsoft world and it is becoming the leading platform.

Most warehouse management systems today offer the user a choice of several database managers, usually including Microsoft SQL and Oracle, but a few are still limited to a single DBMS. Since DBMS licensing is required in addition the warehouse management system license, use of an existing database manager license can reduce the cost of a project and is therefore worth considering.

Real time or batch options

The earliest warehouse management systems relied heavily on portable batch terminals and thus were not real-time, despite online access through desktop terminals. Today, virtually all warehouse management systems support RF terminals that give all operators online access and thus support real time data. Some systems, however, also provide optional support for the older portable batch terminals.

There are two advantages to batch terminals. First, they area significantly less expensive and their use eliminates the need for an RF network in the warehouse. This cost difference can be important, especially in smaller warehouses. And second, batch terminals can work in the rare instances in which RF communication cannot be used, either due to RF interference, radio wave propagation issues, or regulatory limitations.

The great majority of warehouse management systems use RF terminals. Batch terminals should not be specified without good reason.

Dealing in the Market Today

Whenever one makes a major purchase, homework is essential. In the case of warehouse management systems, it helps significantly to understand the market and the suppliers. The following is necessarily interpretive, but should be of value, especially during the proposing and contracting phases.

Supplier Tiers

Conventional thinking has dividend the warehouse management system market into three tiers of suppliers. While there is no official or legal definition of the tiers, the concept is useful.

The top level (tier 1) consists[32] of four suppliers who provide the highest level of functionality and service and who command the highest prices. Tier 1 systems are typically aimed at and address the highest-volume warehouses.

- SAP (*www.sap.com*) dominates the market for firms that use SAP's enterprise requirements software (ERP). It's Logistics Execution System (LES), has improved significantly in recent years.
- Manhattan Associates (*www.manh.com*) is the largest of the specialized warehouse management system suppliers. It has historically been the most successful supplier of best-of-breed software and has the largest number of working installations. Manhattan is publicly traded (Nasdaq; MANH).
- Red Prairie (*www.redprairie.com*) was previously known as McHugh-Freeman Associates. The company is privately held. It has systems optimized for both large and small warehouses and has a large number of successful installations.
- High Jump (*www.highjumpsoftware.com*) was for some years a wholly owned subsidiary of 3M, which presumably gave it access to significant funding. Now privately held, the company is the youngest of the tier 1 suppliers, but has been successful and has quality references.

Tier 2 companies tend to be are smaller and to have less fully developed software which, despite some feature shortcomings, may still have all of the capabilities needed for a specific industry. Tier 2 companies tend to price their products below the tier 1 suppliers.

---

[32] Tier definitions are presented from the viewpoint of this writer. Others may differ in their definitions. Further, the supplier list almost certainly will change over time.

There are dozens of tier 2 warehouse management system suppliers. Examples include:

- Accellos (*www.accellos.com*)
- Cadre Technologies (*www.cadretech.com*)
- CDC Software (*www.cdcsupplychain.com*)
- HK Systems (*www.hksystems.com*)
- Infor (*www.infor.com*)
- Logility (*www.logility.com*)
- Robocom Systems International (*www.robocom.com*)
- Sterling Commerce (*www.sterlingcommerce.com*)
- Swisslog (*www.swisslog.com*)
- Zethcon (*www.zethcon.com*)

Tier 3 companies tend to be more recent start-ups together with a few companies that sell warehouse management systems as a sideline along with other software, material handling equipment, or other products. Some tier 3 systems were purchased from third parties for resale, while others are newly developed. Other tier 3 firms have been in the business longer and have more mature software, but for one reason or another do not have tier 1 or tier 2 status.

Tier 3 systems tend to address smaller warehouses and tend to have less capacity. They also tend to omit the more sophisticated features and to concentrate on the basics, but tier 3 licenses are usually available at much lower cost, making them viable competitors for some installations. On the other hand, being more recent, tier 3 firms tend to be the technology leaders. Their software is the newest and thus is based on the most recent platforms, use the newest and best tools, and support cutting edge hardware.

There are far too many tier 3 companies to even begin to list them.

These lists do not constitute recommendation of any firm or firms. Over the years, several trade publications have reviewed warehouse management systems in detail and have published comparison grids and other studies. The reader is referred to these publications (and, of course, to the companies themselves) for more information.

Current Development

The decades of the 1980s and 1990s and the first few years of the 21st century amounted to a function/feature race between the warehouse management system suppliers. That race, now, is basically over (with no clear winner). Although function and feature enhancement continues and new software versions continue to be introduced, the tier 1 suppliers (and many of the tier 2 suppliers) can be considered fully functioned.

Recent development has concentrated on suites of peripheral (but valuable) tools, especially in the areas of optimization and analysis.

Warehouse management systems have long been oriented toward managing and optimizing the work inside a single warehouse, for the most part without reference to either other company warehouses (the horizontal aspect of the supply chain) or customer/supplier warehouses (the vertical aspect), or to transportation issues. While these applications have had great benefit, from the viewpoint of the total supply chain, they suboptimize.

Optimization improvements now being developed in leading warehouse management systems to aim at total system coordination and global optimization. They view all system inventories from existing production schedules, to material in transit, to warehouse inventories, and to store or distributor inventories. They analyze inventories in light of known or forecast demand, define production and/or product purchase plans, warehouse transfers and demand service strategies (or inventory allocations). One supplier reports inventory reductions of 11 to 15%[33]. The thrust of these enhancements comes from the coordination of warehouse management systems with transportation management systems and manufacturing execution systems so they work together, rather than independently.

Business intelligence, on the other hand, implies improved visibility into all elements of the supply chain, providing analyses and data that are configurable, meaningful to the individual manager, and generated in real time. On-demand analyses, ad-hoc reporting, and remote alerts and alarms are all included.

---

[33] Manhattan Associates as reported in Modern Materials Handling magazine.

Other Considerations

Successful dealing in the warehouse system marketplace also requires an understanding of a few other things. Some may be obvious, but all bear repeating.

- ➢ All but the smallest warehouse management system suppliers employ separate sales and installation teams. The sales people you deal with, therefore, will be replaced when you sign the contract. This means that you should insist on meeting a company's project manager before judging its capabilities.

- ➢ In recent years the warehouse management system market has matured and the saturation point has been reached. Times have thus gotten tough for the suppliers. One result has been a number of mergers, buyouts and refinancing deals. Some suppliers are selling code that was originally written many years ago by people who have not worked for the company or its predecessor companies for a very long time. In some cases, this can affect supportability. In other cases, code structure may be partially obsolete, making some features awkward and hard to use at the lowest levels. In other cases, code may be inefficient.

- ➢ Because the economic cost of entry into the warehouse management system business is low, new suppliers and new systems appear on the market frequently. Their survival rate is typical of new startup businesses, which means that the firm looking for a warehouse management system must do its due diligence to assure that they are dealing with a supplier who will be around in the years to come to provide support. Even long-established suppliers may be in poor financial condition, making due diligence even more important.

Buying a WMS

As was observed earlier in this paper, the warehouse management system purchase project is structurally little different from the project needed to make any major software purchase. However, there are important details and comments that can be made at lower levels that both project managers and executives will find useful. This section concentrates on those items.

The project itself, beginning with the initial concept and ending with system startup, is shown at the right in Figure 20. Each of the tasks shown in the figure is described in more detail in the pages that follow.

While shown as a linear process, execution is rarely that simple. Tasks overlap. Work must be updated or redone. And opportunities abound to use dead time by working ahead. Nevertheless, the figure provides a general structure and a reasonable basis for discussion in this paper.

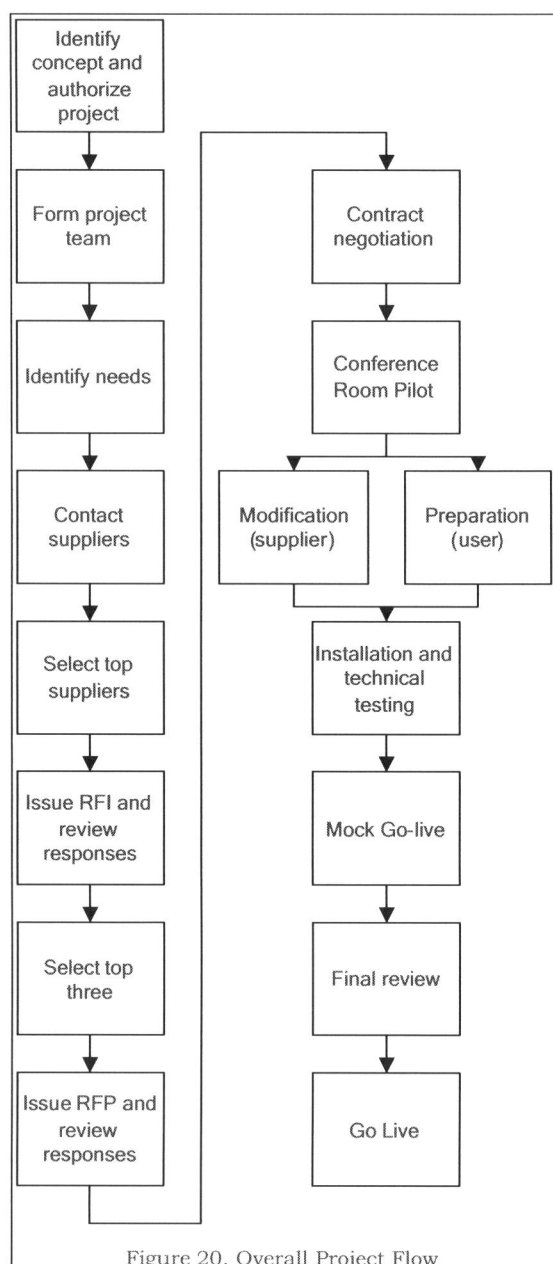

Figure 20. Overall Project Flow

Identify Concept

The original idea to install or replace a warehouse management system may surface during lunch, as part of a meeting on another subject, or while reading trade publications or attending a trade show. Regardless of where the idea came from, it probably was discussed by several people and informally validated, possibly by research in the trade press or by discussions with people in other firms who have been through the project. At this point there is an idea that the project would benefit the company and the proponents might even have a rough idea of the costs and project ROI, but probably do not have much detail.

The first step should be to recognize that even an exploratory project would cost both time and money. Senior management, therefore, will rightly ask for justification before giving permission to form a team and begin work on the details[34]. Justification at this level is likely to be very informal since out-of-pocket costs (costs other than labor) will probably be limited to some travel expenses. But, regardless of the degree of formality, a conscious decision to undertake a warehouse management system evaluation should be made, and that decision should be made by and supported by senior management because of the cross-functional nature of the resources required.

Justification of the evaluation project is probably best done by study.

- The trade press can provide a number of success stories and analyses, possibly some in similar businesses.
- Professional societies[35] provide networking opportunities and contacts that can help.
- Initial vendor contacts can also provide data (although some companies may wish to defer these contacts until later in the process)
- Colleges and Universities with Supply Chain or Logistics curricula may provide perspective
- This briefing provides a description of the team required (see below). Total work hours required for a system evaluation and justification can run from a few hundred in a small firm to a few thousand in a large and complex supply chain.

---

[34] If the original proponents of the project are members of senior management, they should ask themselves the same question.
[35] Notably the Warehouse Education and Research Council (*www.werc.org*) and the Council for Supply Chain Management Professionals (*www.cscmp.org*)

Form Project Team

With management support and encouragement in place, your warehouse management system project should be the responsibility of a project team, headed by a designated project manager. The same team should manage the project from initial concept through final installation and a subset of the team should retain ongoing responsibility for the system after installation.

The project team should consist of no less than four and no more than eight people. Very small teams tend to lack expertise and experience, while very large teams quickly become unwieldy, political and therefore inefficient. In very large organizations, the regular team members can be supplemented by supporting members who contribute as needed from the sidelines.

The choice of team members should consider a number of factors.

- Someone who is technical enough to understand system internals and the implications of technical decisions should represent the information technology organization.

- Someone senior enough to have experience dealing with software suppliers should also be drawn from the information technology organization.

- Someone who knows warehouse operations, methods and procedures in extensive detail should represent the user community. If possible, actual experience working as a material handler or a supervisor is valuable. In some instances, two or three users at this level can be profitably included on the team[36].

- Someone who knows the warehouse and how it works from the management level should be part of the team.

The team leader should be chosen from the team membership, with the single most important consideration being leadership capabilities coupled with a personal attitude of eagerness and desire to see the project through to success. Given these qualities, however, if all other important factors are equal, leadership should probably be drawn from the user group rather than from information technology.

---

[36] We know of at least one instance in which senior hourly people were included in the system selection process. With the right people, there can be great advantage in terms of bringing the team down to earth and winning acceptance of the system on the warehouse floor.

Any good warehouse management system installation has a fundamental impact on the way you and your organization do business. It affects the daily working routines of lots of people. Information technology people often understand this, but simply don't know enough about day-to-day life in the pits to do a good job of calling the shots. Since project managers call a lot of shots, they should be drawn from the user organization.

> At one company, an administrative services unit staffed with talented people managed a warehouse management system installation project. The user organization was involved, but was located 200 miles from the administrative services organization. Because administrative services had immediate access to top management, they got to make most of the decision.
>
> The system installation went smoothly and, from a technical viewpoint, there were very few problems. But the user manager hadn't mentally accepted responsibility for the project and hadn't done his homework. A physical rearrangement of the facilities, which was essential for the smooth operation of the system, hadn't even been started by the time the installation date arrived. Although the hardware and software met all specifications, and was successful in every way from the supplier's viewpoint, the system was not placed in service until new user management could be hired and trained.

Independent consultants can serve a purpose on a warehouse management installation project team by filling gaps in available expertise and by providing experience that does not exist within the organization. The designation of a consultant as team leader, however, should be done only under very limited circumstances. The consultant must be known and trusted, must be willing to enter into a long-term project with assurances that continuity will be preserved, and must be compensated in such a way that he or she is accountable for results.

Committees

The difference between a project committee and a project team is this: a committee makes decisions by voting, while a team makes decisions by consensus with the project manager ruling by fiat when consensus cannot be reached.

Committees aren't efficient. Give your project manger the support and staff necessary together with the power to make decisions on behalf of everyone else. If absolutely necessary, use a committee but keep the membership as small as possible. Limit committee membership to people who are committed to making the system work and to completing the project on time and within budget.

> More than ten copies of a large and complex warehouse management system were installed nationwide in a Fortune 100 company a few years ago. The company named a project manager, but failed to give him adequate authority. As a result, project meetings were too big for the customer's available conference rooms and had to be held in a rented hall (literally). The simplest decision took weeks to make and the project was several hundred thousand dollars more expensive than it had to be.

If you can't find anyone in your organization who you are willing to trust with project management responsibility you may not be paying your people enough and, therefore, not attracting the best possible people. Project management is a tough job. It takes talented, dedicated, and well-paid people.

Identify Needs

Classical project management theory says that the identification of needs (or requirements) should be done by interviews with the people who will have contact with the system. The gathering of ideas is important, but for warehouse management system projects, should be supplemented with ideas from other sources, especially from people with relevant experience.

The key to creating an effective list of requirements is management of the level of detail involved. Each requirement should be business-based in the sense that there should be a valid business reason for it, but there are also requirements that are real, but are difficult to assign to a business reason. Further, there are business reasons that, if driven into too much detail, become unnecessarily complex technical requirements. In effect, a balancing act is required. It is a matter of determining what is needed, but with enough flexibility to allow different systems to fill the needs in different ways.

For example, one prospective customer comes to mind that very much wanted product recall capabilities. In support of the recalls, the customer specified that serial numbered product moving through the warehouse had to be tracked on a piece-by-piece basis. In fact, the real requirement had nothing to do with serial number tracking before shipment and the customer's over-specification significantly increased quoted system costs.

The project team should identify needs in three specific areas: system function, system interfaces, and system technology. The team should also consider, even at this early stage, a variety of installation methodologies to assure that suppliers can effectively support the project all the way to the end.

Functional Requirements

Functional requirements should be gathered from system users, but should be filtered or interpreted by people who understand how warehouse management systems work and what they can and cannot accomplish.

Another source of requirements can be found in this briefing, especially in the section titled Warehouse Management Systems starting on page 3 where features and functions are listed and discussed.

Independent consultants with expertise in warehouse management systems may also be able to contribute ideas and critique requirements lists.

Interface Requirements

Required system interfaces are also important and should be defined along with other requirements. These interfaces should operate unattended to a schedule defined by the user. Because volume can be significant, they are usually implemented as batch file transfers, but the frequency of transfer can be as little as every few minutes. Where real business requirements exist, implementation as real-time (record by record) interfaces is possible.

- Host system interfaces. Virtually every warehouse management system interfaces to one or more business hosts. Data exchanged includes downloads from the host to the warehouse management system:

  - Item and bill of material data including new item additions to the catalog or bill of materials, item descriptive, dimensional and weight data, item packaging data, UPC codes, and ultimately, item cancellations.

- Purchase or supplier orders including items, quantities, due dates, supplier numbers and more

- Inbound ASNs and loads defining order numbers, content and expected arrival date

- Customer or shipping orders including items, quantities, due dates, customer numbers, carriers, priorities, messages or instructions, and more

- Customer, carrier and vendor data including names and addresses, contact information, credit limits, preferred carriers and more

- Inventory locations and quantities[37]

Data uploaded from the warehouse management system to the business host system(s) includes:

- Actual receipts and/or quantities put away, used to relieve inbound orders and maintain host inventories

- Actual shipments, used to relieve customer orders and maintain host inventories

- Inventory adjustments, together with reason codes and other information

- Inventory holds and releases, again with reason codes and other information

- Summarized inventory status, used by the host systems as necessary to re-set inventory values

➢ Other system interfaces. Many warehouse management system installations also feature interfaces with non-host systems such as:

- Appointment scheduling and yard management systems

- Transportation management and manifesting systems

- Slotting systems

---

[37] Inventories are maintained by the warehouse management system and uploaded to the host(s), but the ability to download inventory values can be very useful at system startup time.

- Labor management systems
- Data mining/analysis/reporting systems

Due to the nature of the data handled, these interfaces are more likely to be real time than are host interfaces

➤ MHE interfaces. Interfaces with automated material handling equipment are common in automated warehouses. These interfaces are usually real-time and are almost always customized[38] to match the custom equipment. The most common interfaces are with:

- Sortation systems. Tote or carton identities and destinations are downloaded to the sortation system and actual deliveries are uploaded to confirm completion.

- Carousels. Groups of work (picks and putaways) are downloaded and confirmations of completion are returned to the warehouse management system. Different carousels support different internal databases[39] and thus require different data.

- Automated Storage and Retrieval Systems (ASRSs). Like carousels, groups of work are downloaded and confirmations of completion are returned.

- Pick-By-Light And Put-To-Light Systems. Groups of work are again downloaded and both confirmations and exceptions are returned. Unlike carousels and ASRSs, the more sophisticated pick-by-light systems allow multiple simultaneous workers.

- Automated Picking Machines (A-frames). Generally automated picking machines deal only with picks; replenishments are handled by the warehouse management system, but separately from the automation.

- Automated Guided Vehicle Systems (AGVs). Material handling unit (pallet) identities are downloaded along with source and destination locations and completion confirmations are returned.

---

[38] Many warehouse management systems have standard MHE interfaces, but they tend to standardize the infrastructure only and require customization to match detailed requirements. Because interfaces are usually customized, the descriptions given here may not match requirements for a specific project.

[39] Some carousel systems may even maintain internal inventories and thus may require item downloads.

- RF system interface. The RF system interface is usually built into the warehouse management system, but should still be considered by the project team because it defines eligible RF system suppliers.

- Human interfaces. Human interfaces for in-house system users are likewise built into the warehouse management system, but the project team should define requirements for access by:

    - Customers. Some businesses find it advantageous to allow customer access into order status and even inventory status.

    - Suppliers. Similarly it may be useful for a business to give suppliers access to orders and to the inventories that they provide.

    - Carriers. Carrier relations can also benefit from access into outgoing order and volume data.

- Data import/export. The ability to export data for other tools (such as spreadsheets) can be important because it can provide management with significant ad-hoc analytical power. Import capabilities are less significant, but can also be useful.

Technical Requirements

The definition of technical system requirements is also important, especially in two areas:

- Platform. The choice of a technical platform is primarily an IT decision based on systems currently being supported and the firm's ability to support a warehouse management system's hardware, operating systems, and networks. Larger and more sophisticated companies can support almost any chosen platform and thus need not spend much time on selection at this point in the process. Smaller firms may wish to limit the platforms in use and, where this is the case, it should be recognized and included in the requirements from the start.

    Generally available platforms in the warehouse management system business include Unix, Microsoft, and less common, AS/400. Other platforms may be available, but will require some searching.

- Database. Warehouse management systems are large and complex real-time systems that, in some cases, support dozens or even hundreds of simultaneous users. They need efficient database managers to provide reasonable response times to users. Database managers, like operating systems, represent significant investment and require support. If a specific database manager is preferred, or if one is ruled out, that should be identified as part of the requirements.

Warehouse management systems are generally available using most of the major database managers. Microsoft SQL and Oracle are the most common. Informix, Sybase and others are also available.

Installation Method

Although it may seem early, this briefing recommends that the project team carefully consider installation methods and determine installation requirements as part of the initial specification effort. The decisions made here will have major impact later and should not be last minute decisions.

There are three major methods of warehouse management system installation:

- Big Bang. The big bang method assumes that all preparation and training is done and then, possibly over a weekend, the data is moved from the old system to the new one, the old system is set aside, and all subsequent production is done with the new system.

  Big bang installations carry a measure of risk, but are also the simplest and most straightforward way of implementing. Risk can be limited with proper planning and pre-established fallback positions, but cannot be eliminated entirely. Despite this risk, big bang is the most commonly used method.

- Phase-in. Warehouse management systems can be phased into operation and the phase-in approach has been successfully used a number of times. Its primary disadvantage is that it significantly increases the duration of the implementation process, potentially increasing implementation cost and delaying benefits for months. While risk is reduced, it is not eliminated and the added complexity of the phase-in approach adds risks of its own.

  In a multi-warehouse environment, phasing-in a new warehouse management system by installing it in one warehouse at a time is an obvious idea. And, in fact, almost all multi-warehouse installations are done one warehouse at a time. Usually the installation process gets more efficient as experience is gained and later installations are much easier and cheaper than early ones.

  Within a single warehouse, phasing in a new warehouse management system is much more difficult than it sounds. Obvious ideas are to initially enable the system in portions of the physical warehouse, or for specific products or product lines, or for specific customers or suppliers and then, over time, extend the system until it ultimately is completely operational. The problem with this scheme is the degree of control that the warehouse management system exercises over the warehouse. If it, for instance, controls the inventory of only one specific product line, there will be difficulties servicing orders that also contain other product lines and managing warehouse space that holds or could hold other product lines.

Phasing, however, has been successfully done from a functional standpoint. A warehouse could, for instance, begin by implementing the receiving and put-away processes, subsequently add picking and shipping, and ultimately complete the system installation with cycle counting, replenishment and the rest. In general, this approach requires custom software to interface the new and old systems so they can work together, but if the details are properly managed, it can and has been done. Whether or not the concurrent reduction in risk justifies the extra work and extra cost is an open question.

- Parallel operation. The idea behind parallel system operation is that the warehouse management system is installed and implemented, but the system being replaced is not deactivated. Instead, both systems are operated in parallel for a time. Only when the new warehouse management system has proven itself, is the old one removed.

  The basic idea behind parallel operation is risk reduction. Because it preserves the old system and gives the user the ability to revert back to the old system with essentially no risk or effort, the promise of low overall risk is great. However, practice has found that the cost of parallel operation is also great. All data must be entered in duplicate and verified in duplicate and the time and effort involved can be prohibitive. Further, there are situations and features (such as MHE communication) where parallel operation is essentially impossible.

  In fact, warehouse management system installation with parallel operation with older systems is done only very rarely. When all the costs are ultimately estimated, the reduction in risk simply does not justify the work involved.

In addition to the basic method, the project team should give thought to the installation process, which is described in more detail starting on page 113. At the minimum, a four-step process should be identified as a system requirement from the beginning:

- Conference room pilot
- Go-live planning

- Mock go-live
- Real go-live

Contact Suppliers and Select Initial Group

With a reasonable start made to defining your system requirements, the next step is to contact software suppliers. The objective of these contacts is the development of an initial supplier list. This briefing suggests that the supplier list start with as many suppliers as possible and then be winnowed through a series of increasingly detailed investigations.

Begin with a review of the requirements and select between three and six that you consider deal breakers – requirements that simply cannot be compromised in any way for any cost. Then telephone or e-mail every warehouse management system supplier you can locate and ask about these deal-breakers. Those who give favorable answers belong on your initial long list; those who do not can be written off.

Examples of some deal-breaker requirements include:

- Ability to handle your transaction volume and number of workers
- Support for a specific computer platform and/or a specific database manager
- Support for specific processes or procedures required, especially those required by a specific industry
- Availability of software support 24/7/365 (if required)
- Multi-lingual capabilities (if required)
- Supplier company size, age and experience, and financial strength measures

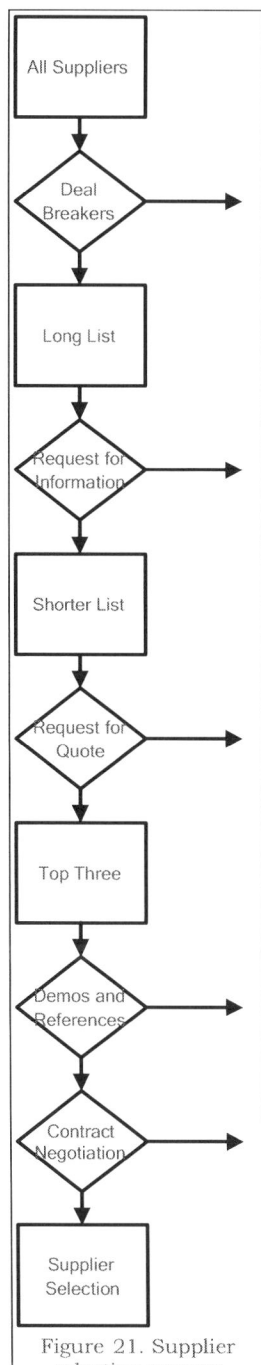

Figure 21. Supplier selection process

Initial supplier contact could result in a list of as many as twenty or twenty-five firms. If the list is significantly longer than that, it might be well to consider additional high-priority requirements and make some follow-up phone calls. Or, if you prefer, you can continue at this stage with a longer list, recognizing that it will entail additional work.

Create and Issue RFI

The project team should next develop a Request For Information (RFI) document for distribution to the suppliers on the initial long list. An RFI is a fast and easy way of getting answers to some basic questions. It is also a way of eliminating suppliers to shorten the list for the more detailed RFQ to come.

The RFI can be a relatively informal document. Attorneys need not be involved. However, because a large number of RFI copies will be sent out, it should be well organized and complete so that the suppliers can respond without inundating the team with questions. A well organized and well written RFI also greatly simplifies the task of evaluating supplier responses.

There is no industry standard format for RFIs. However, the document should, at the minimum, include:

- An introduction describing your company and the content and purpose of the document. This introduction should include a statement of your supplier selection process including the fact that a more detailed Request For Quotation will follow.

- A specific request that the supplier respond in writing, complete with a due date for the response and a process for the supplier to follow if the due date cannot be met. Due dates should be no less than two weeks after receipt of the document, and more time should be allowed if the RFI is long and complicated.

- A list of contact people including names, titles, telephone numbers, e-mail addresses and postal addresses.

- A statement of the purposes of the warehouse management system project and the benefits expected.

- A description of the facility (or facilities) where the warehouse management system will be installed including size, location and any special characteristics.

> A recapitulation of the deal-breaker requirements used to develop the initial supplier list, together with a request that the supplier re-confirm that its software will meet these requirements.

> A list of the most important of your detailed requirements, as best the team knows them at the time[40]. This list should include a place for the suppler to respond (a) supported in the current version, (b) supportable with customization, or (c) not supported.

The RFI does not ask for cost information, but is entirely centered on system and supplier capabilities. There may be value in asking the suppliers for a typical system cost – or for the cost of a comparable and recently installed system, but we haven't yet reached the point where the supplier knows enough about your company to do more and costing isn't the point of the RFI.

Spell check your RFI and make it look as professional as you reasonably can. Then send a copy to every system supplier on the list and wait for responses. Despite the informal or semi-formal nature of the RFI, an effort should be made to treat all suppliers equally at this stage, particularly in terms of the amount of time they are given to respond.

A little understanding of the RFI and RFQ process from the supplier's viewpoint may help. Larger companies may regularly receive several of these documents per week. They have full time staff that does nothing by respond to them, largely using prewritten boilerplate. Each document, however, must be individually read and studied in detail to assure that the boilerplate is appropriate and responsive to your questions. Changes to the boilerplate often require management approval, as will the completed response to you.

The fact that this document is an RFI and does not require detailed quotation makes the job of the responder easier and thus promotes a better quality and better crafted response, which is what is wanted at this stage.

Subsequent to the issuance of the RFI, suppliers will call with questions and will, of course, maneuver to put themselves in the most favorable possible light. Listen to what they have to say and provide the information they ask for. Remember, however, that if you give one supplier something important that wasn't included in the RFI document, it is only fair to see that all other suppliers receive the same advantage.

You should consider yourself obligated to hold detailed information about the suppliers confidential, regardless of whether or not a written agreement is signed. However, some suppliers may ask that you sign an agreement before

---

[40] It is probably best to exclude requirements that you consider optional or negotiable from the RFI. Responses to a short RFI are much easier to evaluate than a long one.

they reply to your RFI. In general, these agreements are routine and, subject to review by an attorney, they should be signed.

Select Short List

Reading and evaluating the responses to an RFI is a significant job. Be sure:

> That the responses do provide the information you asked for

> That there are no terminology issues that could have caused the supplier to misunderstand your need or could cause you to misunderstand the response

> That you do, in fact, actually understand the supplier's answers.

Don't hesitate to discuss the RFI and the responses to it with the suppliers.

Don't be surprised if no supplier meets all of your requirements.

This briefing suggests the use of a matrix format for the evaluation of RFI responses. Put the suppliers in columns and the features and other questions you asked in rows and then briefly summarize each response in the matrix cells. It is also possible to assign numeric values to the response cells and compute a rating for each supplier as a guide to their evaluation, but at times this can be harder than it sounds and numeric evaluations should be tempered with good business judgment.

Using the results of the RFI, pare your list of suppliers down to something between five and ten firms, selecting those firms that appear to have systems which can best meet your requirements. These are the firms to which Requests for Quotation (RFQs) will be sent. Like the RFI responses, those that come in response to your RFQ will probably contain surprises, so at least five firms are necessary. On the other hand, the analysis of RFQ responses is even more demanding than the RFI, so the list should be as short as possible.

The analysis of RFI responses and the recommendation of firms to stay on your supplier list are jobs that can be outsourced to a consultant, especially if the consultant has experience that can add value.

Create and Issue RFQ

With the shortened list complete, the next step is to expand on the RFI in the form of a formal Request for Quotation (RFQ).

Unless your situation is unusual, you will have learned quite a bit about the market and the suppliers (and about warehouse management systems) from the responses to your RFI. Therefore, the first step in creating your RFQ is to revisit your requirements. Be sure they all continue to make sense in the context of your business and that they do, in fact, actually reflect your true business needs. Rewrite where necessary.

The RFQ Document

Significant portions of your RFQ can be lifted from your RFI document with appropriate modifications. This saves a good deal of work in re-writing. Sections that can be copied after updating include:

➤ An introduction describing your company and the content and purpose of the document.

➤ A specific request that the supplier respond to your RFQ in writing and that the supplier's response include pricing details and a delivery schedule. Due dates for the response should be established and, like the RFI, should be no less than two weeks after receipt of the document the supplier's office.

➤ A list of contact people including names, titles, telephone numbers, e-mail addresses and postal addresses.

➤ A statement of the purposes of the warehouse management system project and the benefits expected.

➤ A description of the facility (or facilities) where the warehouse management system will be installed including size, location and any special characteristics.

➤ A recapitulation of the deal-breaker requirements used to develop the initial supplier list, together with a request that the supplier re-confirm that its software will meet these requirements.

➤ A recapitulation of the requirements put forth in the RFI, requesting that the supplier reconfirm its responses as part of its response to the RFQ. If possible, it is elegant to include each supplier's individual RFI responses in his or her copy of the RFQ (thus holding them to their words), but that involves significant clerical work and may not be practical in all cases.

New sections to be added into the RFQ document include:

➢ A list of all requirements (both the firm one and the negotiable ones) not included in the RFI, together with a request that the supplier state individually whether these requirements can be met with the base software, will require modification, or will not be achievable.

➢ A request for a list of the individual system modifications needed, describing and specifying the purpose of each. The suppliers should also describe how the system would function if the modification were not done.

➢ A structure for the supplier's financial response that requests a cost breakdown in whatever way you see fit. In general, it makes sense for you to ask the suppliers to:

- Separate license fees from other costs
- Individually quote all license fees required and specify which licenses you will need to purchase separately
- Individually quote all hardware required, indicating whether the system supplier will provide the hardware or whether it must be purchased separately.
- Break labor cost quotations into installation cost, training cost, system modification cost, and project management cost.
- Include support costs (usually annual fees), specifying the additional cost of supporting each modification separately.
- Specify software modifications individually, providing a separate cost for each.
- Separate estimated travel expense reimbursement from other costs
- Specify payment terms and late payment penalties. Also, international suppliers should be asked to specify payment currencies.

➢ A statement that all quotations must be held valid for at least ninety days or, if a supplier is unwilling to hold his or her bid open that long, that the supplier specifically state an expiration date.

➢ A requirement that the suppliers explicitly state any and all warranties offered.

➢ Notification to the suppliers that they will be asked to provide system demos on site in your offices, that they will be asked to provide a site visit at an existing customer site, that they will be asked to provide additional telephone references, and that they will be asked to introduce you to the specific individuals who will lead (and, possibly, work on) your project. The RFQ should not ask that these due diligence items be provided with the written response, but should ask only that the written response include acknowledgement from the suppliers that they can and will be provided on request[41].

➢ A requirement that the supplier provide a description of its user group (if there is one), together with a measure of the degree to which current system users participate in it.

➢ A requirement that the supplier enclose a sample license agreement (along with all other required agreements) as part of their response.

➢ A request that suppliers include statements of their financial condition with their responses. Some suppliers (primarily those that are privately held) will resist. All the RFQ can do is serve notice to the suppliers that failure to respond will be considered similar to evidence that the supplier is in poor or marginal financial shape.

Unlike the Request for Information, a Request for Quote is a formal document with legal implications. You are asking your suppliers to provide legally binding quotations. Therefore, review of the completed document by an attorney before sending it out is a good idea.

Do one last spell check on the RFQ before mailing it. Expect numerous calls and questions from the short list suppliers. And, as was suggested with the RFI, remember that you have an ethical obligation to treat the suppliers equally, so facts that come to light in discussions with one supplier should be shared with all.

Some warehouse management system buyers schedule bidder meetings in which all of the competitors meet in a group with the company's project leader. In this meeting, the suppliers receive an oral introduction to the company and the project, are given a physical tour of the warehouse, and have an opportunity to ask questions. The theory behind bidders' meetings is that all suppliers will have the same information and will therefore provide comparable quotations.

---

[41] Even the largest warehouse management system suppliers have only a limited number of customers who are willing to spend the time and money to be a reference site. The suppliers have a legitimate concern about over-using these references and you, as a potential customer, also should be concerned about what you will be asked to do as a future reference site. It is thus reasonable that references be requested only at the very end of the process, and then only from the firms that actually have a chance of getting your business.

Bidders meetings have pros and cons. On the positive side, these meetings may clear up misunderstandings and they generally do improve the consistency of the bidding process. On the negative side, however, remember that information coming from a supplier to the company is automatically shared with the supplier's competitors. The savviest suppliers will, therefore, ask few questions, preferring to hold those questions for a private phone call to be made later. In general, extremely formal bidding processes and bidders meetings are not advised for commercial firms. They are generally necessary only when corporate policy demands a very formal policy, or when the buyer is a government entity and is required by law, policy or regulation to be formal.

In some rare instances, a supplier might contend that the stated requirements are too complex for bidding without detailed study and might propose a paid project to study the requirements in more detail. Such projects are problematic. Suppliers generally like them when they can get them because not only are they paid for producing at least part of their proposal, but also because the study gives them an inside track on the main system installation project. In general, if only one supplier seems to be having trouble quoting a particular requirement, a paid study can be declined.

On the other hand, all such suggestions should be considered. The subject of the confusion should be explored with other suppliers and, if there is indication that unanticipated complexity or uncertainty exists, additional work is needed. Whether that work is done internally, through a system supplier study, or by an independent consultant is a question of judgment. Regardless of who does the work, however, such an issue will almost certainly represent a major delay in the supplier selection process, so it should be considered carefully.

Evaluating Proposals

Proposals responding to a warehouse management system RFQ will range up from as little as twenty pages to as much as a hundred pages or more. Their evaluation will, in itself, be a significant job.

- ➢ Begin by reviewing the suppliers' responses to your specific requirements. Be certain that the supplier understood your requirements and that you understand its responses. Update and extend the response matrix that you built when evaluating RFI responses.

- ➢ Review the suppliers' list of proposed system modifications and verify that they are reasonably consistent with your expectations.

- ➢ Fold vendor pricing back into your cost justification model, modifying the model as necessary to reflect actual quotations. A separate copy of the model may be required for each supplier. Based on these models, calculate the payback period (or ROI) separately for each supplier.

- In light of the ROI calculations, review the proposed modifications again. For each, assume momentarily that you will buy from the supplier and, determine whether or not the modification enhances the project ROI, or detracts from it when compared to the alternative of doing without the modification. If the modification detracts from the project ROI, remove it from consideration (and contact the supplier to validate your change to his or her quote).

Expect some degree of waffling on delivery dates. The suppliers have no real knowledge of when their contracts will be signed and no certain knowledge of how many other jobs will be signed before then.

Finally, recognize that most suppliers made assumptions both consciously and unconsciously as they wrote your proposal. The better suppliers will provide a separate list of assumptions for you to validate, but if no such list is provided, it is a good idea for the team to review each proposal one more time to develop its own list. Those assumptions, then, should be discussed and validated and any that are obviously incorrect should be discussed with the supplier and the supplier should be given a (relatively short) time to update its proposal.

Final Supplier Selection

Based on work completed to this point, the project team should select at least two and no more than four suppliers to proceed into the final selection process. This choice should be based on the team's ROI calculations and its joint subjective feel for the supplier's capabilities and integrity.

Suppliers on the final list should be contacted and asked to:

- Provide a formal system demonstration in your office. The demo should be scripted so that it concentrates on the subjects of interest to your firm, but also allows the supplier to show other feature and function that he or she thinks may be of value. You should provide the supplier with a demo script, allow several weeks for the supplier to organize the demo and make travel arrangements, and allow between two to four days in a conference room for each supplier to accomplish the demo. (See the discussion on page 110 for more information about scripted demos.)

  When you request the system demonstration, you should also ask that the supplier's project team leader and as many team workers as possible be present. During the demo, you should get to know and evaluate these people to the extent possible, since they will be key to the immediate success of the installation.

- Arrange for a site visit to a warehouse currently running the system you are considering. This site visit should be made during warehouse working hours and should be hosted by the user. You should ask that the visit be made to a company as similar to yours as possible, but should not ask to visit a site in your own industry.

  Expect to travel significant distances for this visit. The additional cost of long distance travel is well worth the benefit of seeing a facility that uses the same system features that you are interested in.

- Provide added telephone references. Like the site visit, telephone references should be selected primarily for their similarity to your operation.

Scripted Demonstrations

In its simplest form, a scripted demonstration is simply a demonstration of the software that concentrates on features and functions of interest to the client. It is pre-planned and is done using a printed agenda.

Scripted demonstrations, however, can be more. If you feel that it is worth the work, most suppliers will be willing to demonstrate using your item table, a selection of your actual customers, suppliers and orders, and logical mockups of at least part of your warehouse and some of your key processes. Demonstrations at this level involve substantial preparation and significant work on your part to gather the data the supplier will need. You must decide whether or not they are worthwhile.

At a minimum, for a vendor to provide a reasonable scripted demo, you must abstract from your requirements list those items that you feel should be demonstrated. As you do this abstraction, remember that the demo itself cannot include any proposed system modifications and also cannot include any interfaces with other systems. These items, of course, will not exist until after the agreements have been signed and the project installation work completed.

Due diligence:

In parallel with the demonstration and reference visit, a certain amount of due diligence research should be done.

First, the project team should look into the financial condition of the proposed supplier. To the extent possible, sources independent of the company should be used. For publicly held companies, this is relatively easy[42]. For privately held ones (most warehouse management system suppliers are private), it can be very difficult. However, your work is not done until you are reasonably sure that you have done everything possible to validate the supplier's stability.

Telephone references should be checked using a structured list of questions developed by the project team (a list of suggested questions appears in Appendix C, starting on page 139). Naturally the references given by the supplier will have been carefully selected by him or her and will be almost entirely favorable and any negative comments made by them should be taken seriously.

One can also ask the supplier's references for the names of additional customers of that supplier. To the extent that names are revealed, an attempt should be made to reach people in those companies who are familiar with the warehouse management system and, especially, with its installation. These people are less likely to be biased in the supplier's favor.

No warehouse management system supplier has a completely successful record and you should not be surprised if you ultimately discover skeletons in closets. The object of the reference call is to look for patterns of dissatisfaction, more than single instances. Customers themselves are likely not without blame.

The site visit should be made by your project leader, one or more members of senior management from your company, and as many team members as possible. You should expect to receive a brief overview of the operation, a tour of the warehouse, a short demonstration of one or two key features of the system, and an opportunity to ask questions. You should go prepared with a list of questions. It is entirely acceptable to ask for a brief meeting with the site's management in private – without the supplier present.

And finally, as part of your due diligence effort, the supplier's proposed agreements should be reviewed by your attorney.

Selection

Supplier selection based simply on price or on ROI is not wise. It should, instead, be very much a judgment call based on a combination of:

- ➢ Financial advantage (ROI) as shown by your justification model using the supplier's quotations

- ➢ Your confidence in his or her ability to get the job done despite obstacles

---

[42] Begin with *http://www.sec.gov/edgar.shtml*

➢ Your determination of the supplier's integrity

Supplier selection should be first made by the project team and recommended to senior management for validation. When the choice has been made, contract negotiations should begin, with the supplier in second place held in abeyance as backup in case the negotiations break down.

Contract Negotiation

After completion of the due diligence work and selection of a single leading supplier, contract negotiations begin. This briefing is not a primer on negotiating techniques, but the following points are worth mentioning:

➢ Your senior management and your attorney should play an active role in the negotiating process. The project leader should act as an advisor to them, but should also be heavily involved. The project leader needs to know about negotiation details because he or she will be responsible for meeting your end of the commitment after the contract is signed.

➢ Everything is on the table including, price, delivery, terms, function and feature, modification, warranties, personnel assignments and much more. If you want something and fail to ask for it, you will certainly not get it.

➢ By this point in time, both you and the supplier have invested substantial time, effort and money in the project. The supplier wants your business. Don't hesitate to be demanding.

➢ On the other hand, you are entering into a long-term relationship with the supplier and it helps a lot if the supplier likes and respects you and your project personnel.

➢ Some system buyers negotiate simultaneously with the top two suppliers and make the final selection only at contract signature time. Others enter negotiation with the number two supplier only if negotiations fail with number one. The difference is primarily a matter of preference or style.

The Installation Project

The installation project for a warehouse management system usually consists of seven major steps, as shown in Figure 22 at the right. The conference room pilot validates the team's understanding of the software. Following its conclusion, the supplier and the project team have preparation work to be done. Then technical installation is done, the go-live process is tested in an exercise called a mock go-live, its results are evaluated and, assuming reasonable success, the system is brought live.

This process may be modified by either the warehouse management team or the supplier and variations on it are acceptable. However, what is described in this briefing is typical and reasonable.

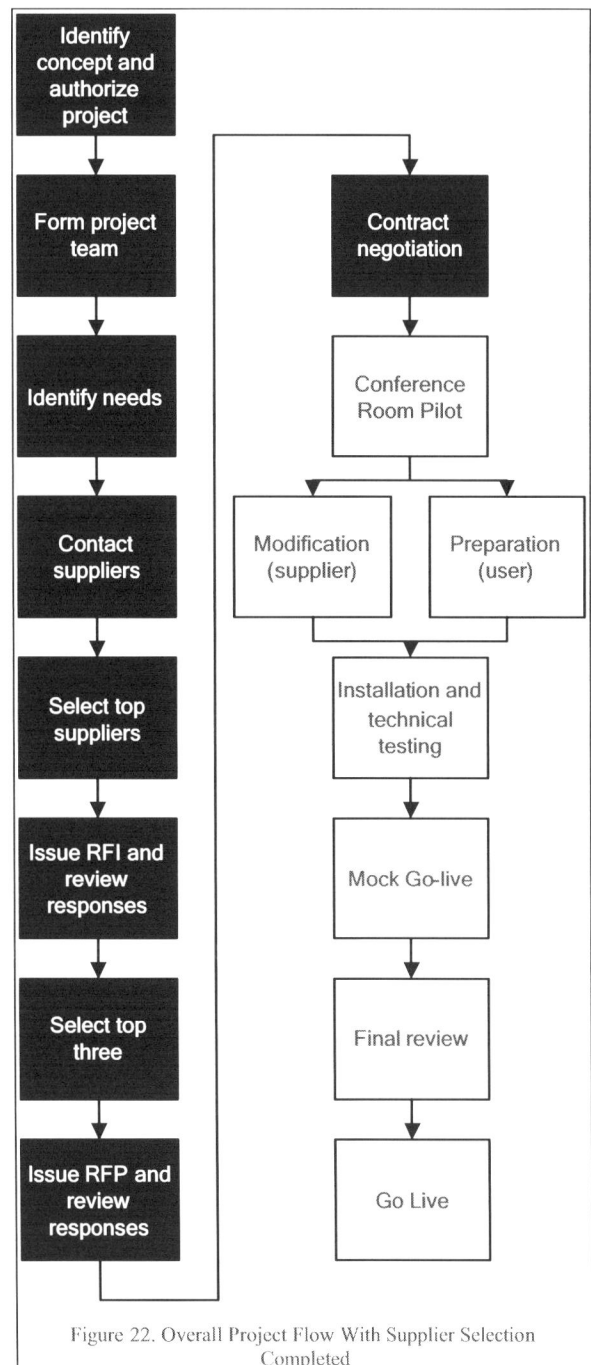

Figure 22. Overall Project Flow With Supplier Selection Completed

Before Installing

The success of a warehouse management system installation cannot be known without some kind of reasonable metrics. If the team's warehouse does not already have satisfactory metrics, they should be put in place and a good set of measurements (or several of them) should be documented before the system goes live. Without metrics in some form, the team will have no way of knowing whether and to what degree the project was a success.

Exactly when metrics are selected and put in place is not terribly important, although a fresh set of measurements should be made very late in the process – usually just before the system is put into actual use.

The metrics to be chosen are beyond the scope of this briefing, but the author offers a separate paper on the subject that may be of help.

Kickoff Meeting

The first step after signature of the license agreements should be a kick-off meeting. Although brief and easily organized (and thus not shown in the process flow chart on the previous page), the kickoff meeting is a critical first step. It should be attended by:

- The entire user project team,
- The supplier's project manager, sales person and key project team members, and
- Senior management from both the user company and the supplier.

Its purpose is to assure project organization and consistency of purpose at a high level from the outset. The meeting is primarily communicative in nature and generally is not intended for decision-making.

The kick-off meeting will last at least four hours and can run into multiple days, but the time spent is well worthwhile. Its agenda should include:

- Introductions of all personnel on both sides including personal backgrounds, responsibilities to the project and desires for the future.
- A presentation by supplier senior management outlining the company organization and the places in that organization held by the other company

personnel present. The manager should also describe the responsibilities and levels of authority given to the people who will work on the project from the supplier's side.

- A presentation by the user company's senior management similarly outlining his or her company's organization and the roles and responsibilities of the people on the installing team. The manager should also describe the background of the project and disclose to the supplier what benefits are expected, how justification was achieved, and how that specific supplier was chosen. This presentation should detail the company's expectations for both the installation project and for the installed system.

- A presentation jointly made by the supplier's sales rep and installation project manager describing how the transition will be managed on the supplier's side.

- A presentation by the supplier's project manager describing the process that will be used to install the system and bring it live. This presentation should include a review of any currently known difficulties and a discussion of the expected timeline. This presentation should specify which company is responsible for which tasks and should lay out the critical path.

- A presentation by the user company's project manager describing the system selection process just completed, detailing the company's plans for use of the system, and discussing the benefits the company expects to receive.

Most successful kickoff meetings are prearranged between the two company's project managers and little is said that they do not already know. There is, however, great value in saying these things publicly in front of both teams and there almost certainly will be new information for at least some of the people present.

Conference Room Pilot

The conference room pilot is, in a sense, an extremely elaborate and detailed system demonstration with extensive hands-on time for users. Its primary purposes are:

➢ To assure that communications between the two teams to this point have been complete and accurate

➢ To validate design of the modifications specified in the agreement before actually starting to commit them to code. (Some modifications may not require validation and can thus be started earlier, but that is a matter of judgment and choice.)

➢ To assure that the completed system will meet the user's needs

The conference room pilot itself occurs in three steps.

The first step is detailed system functional training, provided by the system supplier for the user's team. This training should concentrate on the supplier's standard system without reference to modification, although the supplier should note the places in the standard system where modification will be made. It can easily last a week. The entire user project team should attend, supplemented with additional people as needed.

As a result of this training, the user's project team should understand:

➢ How the system works

➢ What the system does and does not do

➢ How key elements of system logic work

➢ How the system controls are configured and how they can be changed

This is an excellent point to introduce one or two senior hourly people to the project and possible even add them to the project team on a permanent basis. Bringing the hourly workforce into the group provides a new down-to-earth viewpoint on the project and can materially help achieve the team's goals. Equally important, it can build acceptance at the hourly level, acceptance that will be critical when the system is finally taken live. The hourly people brought into the training and subsequent project work should be well experienced, respected by their peers on the floor, and worthy of the status this will give them.

Following the training, or in parallel with it, the supplier should define the data required to load the system, the user should prepare, cleanse and ship this data, and the supplier should loads it into the system (usually done in the supplier's office). The list of data required may be extensive, but certainly will include an item table; an inventory table, a location table (if one exists), inbound and outbound order tables and sufficient supplementary information (such as a warehouse layout drawing) to allow the supplier to create a preliminary configuration.

The third step is what is sometimes called the actual conference room pilot. This exercise is done in a conference room with the supplier's system and the user's real data. It differs from the training in that it is much more oriented toward modifications and toward hands-on experience for the user team.

Most conference room pilots cover all features and functions of the software (or at least all that are proposed for use), demonstrating the system in detail as the work proceeds. Selected areas may be covered briefly, but where modifications are proposed or where there is controversy or discussion over how the system can best be used, they should be very detailed. Each modification should be discussed in detail, delving into screen mockups, logic flowcharts, report layouts and other details as the people attending think necessary. Some companies have videotaped their conference room pilots and have thought the videos very valuable later. Others have felt that a dedicated note-taker is sufficient. Either way, the discussions, any decisions made and any plans for action should be documented.

Some of the modifications may be confirmed or changes may be specified to them during the conference room pilot; others will require additional work by one or the other of the teams, to be handled after completion of the pilot. It is also possible that a need for additional, new modifications will be found.

Each modification should also be rated on criticality by the team with input from the supplier's team. The objective of this rating is to make sure that the modification is essential and that the system cannot be installed without it. Some modifications can be deferred to a later time at relatively little additional cost, while others involve deep infrastructure changes and are much more costly if done later. The advantage of deferral is additional assurance that the modification is really needed. If the user invests in a modification, and later decides that it is not needed, there will be additional costs associated with removing it. If, however, the user defers a modification and later decides that it is essential, the added cost of deferral may easily be justified. So, some measure of skepticism is usually a good thing.

Ultimately, the result of the conference room pilot should be a letter from the user's project manager to the supplier's project manager outlining approval of the modifications and, where necessary, defining the changes and/or additions required. Changes and additions, if any are specified, may require re-quotation by the supplier and a new cycle of approvals at the user's company, but this exercise is far better than dealing with a poorly specified or poorly understood modification after it is installed.

In parallel with all this functional work runs a technical path, which is usually simpler and less complex. It generally consists of several meetings between user and supplier technical personnel to define details of the system's interfaces. These meetings can also involve third parties, especially when host business systems are outsourced or when automated material handling equipment is involved. They can be still more extensive when the system's source code has been licensed and/or when the user company is planning to do more than first-line support internally.

Modification and Preparation

Following the conference room pilot, the user team and the supplier team separate and each goes its own way (although frequent communication between the project managers is certainly advisable to assure that everything stays on schedule and within budget).

During this time, the supplier team orders hardware and equipment and does the detailed design, coding and unit and system testing of the required modifications. In parallel, the user team does any site preparation needed, prepares system data, and either does or directs needed modifications to the host business systems.

On the supplier's side, warehouse management system installations are the company's business. On the user's side, however, the project is peripheral to the business and, therefore, there can be a tendency for work to be set aside when other issues come up. Project managers must diligently control the schedule if everything is to be ready on time.

Testing should not be limited to the warehouse management system, but should also include interfaces and should cover modifications made by the user to host business systems. Interface testing requires coordination between the two teams and may be complex because the host systems are live and the tests must recognize the fact that they are running the business on a day-to-day basis.

Interfaces with automated material handling equipment (carousels, sortation systems and the like) are also hard to test for similar reasons. The teams should work together to develop a test strategy that both assures proper functioning of the interfaces and simultaneously accommodates the needs of the business.

While the supplier is busy with modifications, the user does site preparation, deals with host system modifications, and prepares data. Data preparation is more complex than might be anticipated. The process, properly done, recognizes that the data will have to be loaded into the warehouse management system twice – once for the mock go-live and then again at a later time "for real." There is thus some justification for the team to work toward automated or semi-automated data transfer processes in favor of manual processes.

The user's data preparation should also recognize that there is both static and dynamic data involved. Static data (such as the item table) can be downloaded a day or two in advance of need and a moratorium can be placed on updating the tables until the interfaces are functioning. Dynamic data (such as inventories and orders), however, cannot be loaded until the very last minute and thus should be as automated as possible.

The user team should also recognize that data cleansing may be critical. Modern warehouse management systems use relational databases and often enforce the integrity of relationships. If, for example, an order contains an item that does not appear on the item table, that order could be rejected. This issue should be explored with the supplier's technical staff to assure that data downloads will be accepted when they are sent. During the initial data loading there is likely to be little time to make detailed data corrections.

Installation

When system modifications are complete and have been well tested, the software is installed on the user's server and is tested to assure that it operates correctly. This installation may be done at the supplier's office, particularly if a new server has been ordered for the system, but can also be done in the user's plant. Doing the work in the supplier's office minimizes disruption to both businesses, but is not always possible.

The installed system is then delivered to the user (if necessary) and members of both project teams begin joint functional testing. Testing at this stage should be extensive, covering the base system, modifications and interfaces. (Base system testing is needed because the modifications may have had an unintended and unanticipated impact on it.)

Mock Go-Live

In a mock go-live, the user and supplier teams actually bring the new warehouse management system up and perform work in the warehouse with it – with the full intention that the product handled be returned to its original location and all records reset before resuming operation with the old systems. The mock go-live involves the hourly workforce and normally takes one very long day to accomplish. It obviously requires a great deal of preparation, but when well done, can make the difference between success and failure in the real go-live.

The process often goes like this:

- Operator training is provided, usually the day before the mock go-live. Since the mock go-live need not involve the entire workforce, only some workers will need to be trained, but all who will take part in the exercise should be included. Some workers who have had no previous exposure to the warehouse management system should be included, in part because this will test the training itself. Even those who have been involved earlier should be trained, because their skills will thus be refreshed.

- On the night before the mock go-live, all systems are backed up; dynamic data is downloaded to the warehouse management system and verified.

- Early in the morning on the day of the mock go-live, a pick wave is built. This pick wave is usually carefully selected to assure that all system function is exercised, but the wave itself is kept reasonably small so it can be accomplished in no more than two hours.

- The chosen hourly workers arrive for work as usual. They log onto the new system and perform their tasks under system direction. Two special conditions are imposed:
    - First, each worker is given a pad of sticky notes. Every time he or she handles material, (a) the source location of the material is handwritten on a note and the note is attached to the material, and (b) a second note is used to record the item number, quantity and placement location of the material. This second note is put into a notebook carried by the worker.
    - And second, outbound over-the-road trucks are not actually loaded or dispatched and no real shipments are made.

- All warehouse functions are exercised including receiving, putaway, replenishment, picking, packing, post-pick value-added processes, cycle counting and whatever else is important to daily operations.

- The supplier and user teams each provide several system experts whose job, for the day, is to walk the floor, monitor progress, and assist the workers with answers to questions and solutions to problems. Technical experts are also provided to monitor the system and correct minor problems if and when they arise.

- Although the mock go-live involves only a portion of the hourly workforce, all supervisors should be included. Their job for the day is two-fold. They should first exercise the supervisory features of the system, asking questions and making critiques as they see fit. And secondly, they should spend time on the floor discussing the system with the workers and gathering impressions.

- When the defined work is complete, the hourly workers use the notebooks that they have carried to return all material to the place where it was originally found. The sticky notes are removed from the material at this time and ultimately are discarded.

- And finally the systems are restored from the backups made the previous evening.

The mock go-live is not concerned with productivity; all involved should be encouraged to take their time, assure that they really understand what is happening, and take notes or report to others any problems found.

A well run mock go-live is a significant effort and can have significant cost, but it is hard to find warehouse management system users who have experienced one and think it unnecessary. Historically, mock go-lives seem to expose major issues somewhere between 25% and 50% of the time. And real go-lives, when preceded by a mock go-live, have a success rate exceeding 95%.

Final Review

On completion of the mock go-live, the warehouse returns to normal operation on the old systems and everyone involved is debriefed. If time is available, the hourly workforce may be debriefed on the same day, but if not, then on the next regular workday.

The debriefs are complied into a consolidated issues list and actions are determined for each issue:

- On minor issues, action can be deferred to leave time for work on more important things

- Workarounds can be defined to resolve some issues. Processes and procedures (and training) should be modified accordingly

- Some issues will require software corrections or fixes

- Some issues will require improvements in training

- And, possibly, some issues will require major action to the point of delaying the real go-live.

The user and supplier project teams, working together, should review the completed issues list, develop a plan, assign responsibilities, and implement the plan.

Go-Live

The real go-live is done after the important items on the list of issues from the mock go-live have been resolved. It is done exactly like the mock go-live, but involving all warehouse workers and full warehouse volume. After an hour or two's operation on the new system, the project teams meet and make the decision to continue or to stop.

If the decision is made to continue, workers are told they can stop using sticky notes and begin loading trucks and making shipments. If, on the other hand, a disaster has occurred, work stops, product is returned to its original location, and the warehouse reverts revert to the old system. Failure will cost a day's production, but under some circumstances, that can be better than continuing in the face of a major problem.

Management should expect productivity to decline following the final go-live because, despite all training, the workforce is still learning the new system. Improvement, however, will begin almost immediately and in a matter of days (or at most weeks), will be back to pre-installation levels. Long-term productivity improvement will then follow as the performance level continues to climb.

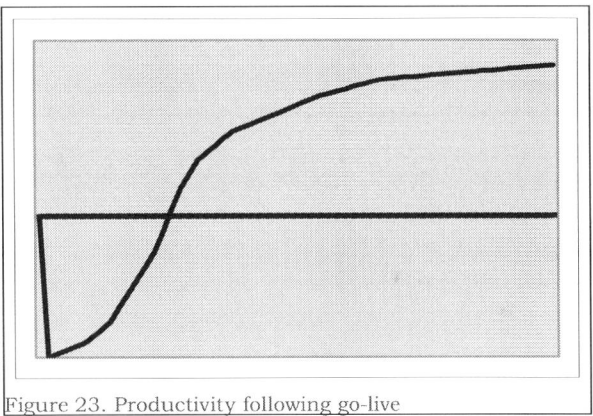
Figure 23. Productivity following go-live

Needless to say, management should plan for a period of low productivity immediately following the system installation and, where necessary, management should consider compensating for it with temporary help and/or in other ways. Businesses with significant seasonality should install warehouse management systems during their slow season.

Ongoing Operation

Following a successful warehouse management system installation, and following the celebratory party that is often the very final responsibility of the project team, most everyone returns to the jobs they had before the idea first surfaced. A few key members of the project team, however, should continue with the system in management and support roles. There is great value in retaining some degree of continuity.

Following the initial learning curve, most warehouse management systems require less than full time support, but three roles are essential and should be specifically included in the responsibilities of whatever people are most appropriate. And, of course, because employees tend to turn over, a backup should be nominated for each role. The three essential roles are:

- Technical
- Operational
- Engineering

All three roles should be defined to include system monitoring and, where necessary, either maintaining the system or initiating maintenance.

Monitoring

Technical system monitoring requires familiarity with the software, hardware, networks and other technical aspects of the system. This role can be outsourced, but many companies prefer to retain at least high-level skills within their organization. The person (or people) responsible should occasionally measure disk utilization, system response time, memory utilization and other technical performance indicators and should be responsible for taking or initiating action when necessary.

The technical system monitor is also usually made responsible for ongoing communication with the supplier's technical support organization.

Operational system monitoring consists largely of two parts. First, the person responsible should continue to watch and critique warehouse metrics. When the numbers (or the trends in the numbers) show a problem, he or she should react. The operational system monitor is the person primarily responsible for altering others if or when it appears that the ultimate system productivity goals have been met or when it becomes apparent that they will not be met.

The second responsibility of the operational system monitor should be to keep in touch with the hourly workforce regarding system use. A well-motivated and loyal workforce is an extremely important source of ideas and valuable feedback and it should not be ignored.

The engineering system monitor has several broad functions. He or she should be responsible for maintaining relations with the system supplier at a management level and for watching (along with the operational monitor) the metrics and system results. He or she should also be charged with keeping in touch with the marketplace and assuring that new developments are considered and, where warranted, evaluated in detail for possible addition to the operation. In addition, the engineering system monitor should be responsible for evaluating ideas and suggestions from the workforce and from the supplier. It is helpful if this person is a trained (and possible degreed) engineer (but with the right person, engineering training can be of secondary importance).

There is also a need to monitor ongoing data integrity and to maintain data cleanliness. This job can be assigned to any of the three monitors, with the assignment best going to the person who is temperamentally most suited and is most interested (and most motivated) in doing the work.

Maintaining

Warehouse management system maintenance involves both routine, repetitive work and occasional one-time projects.

- The system supplier may specify or recommend periodic maintenance practices such as database reorganizations, system backups, purges and the like. In some systems, this work is automated, but even then, someone should watch to assure that the automated processes function properly.

- Many system suppliers provide occasional software patches that should be installed as soon after their issuance as possible. Some suppliers will routinely use remote connections to apply these patches, while others will rely on knowledgeable users to do them locally.

- A routine program of system training is needed, both for new employees and to refresh and extend the skills of existing ones.

- And finally, warehouse slotting depreciates over time and, as a result, productivity will have a tendency to decline. Re-slotting, therefore, is an ongoing job and one that should be done as often as makes sense for the business.

Extending Value

Inherent in the installation of most warehouse management systems is the idea that the system itself changes the way the user does business, changes the user's view of how the business could and should work, and creates new ideas. Therefore, there is an ongoing opportunity to extend the system's value with changes in system configuration or application, or with functional extension of the system. Ideas, in other words, come up that have never before been considered and in the spirit of continuous improvement, they demand evaluation.

Here is a suggested approach:

> A formal systems audit should be done every year or two.

   The audit should review system use and warehouse operations in general. It should look for wasted effort and for ways that the system could be used or extended to eliminate waste. It should examine workarounds and determine their continuing necessity. It should consider the state of user training. It should examine unresolved technical issues and evaluate the state of system hardware including any possible need for replacements. It should consider existing and possible future system interfaces and the value of improving them. And finally, without doing a major evaluation, it should consider other competing systems available in the marketplace and identify opportunities.

   Systems audits are sometimes best done by an independent third party, both because only a third party is likely to have sufficient objectivity and because only a third party will have the uninterrupted time to get the work done promptly. The system auditor, however, needs significant knowledge of the specific warehouse management system in use and this may argue that the supplier itself is best qualified. (Of course, the system supplier is the wrong source for an independent look at the software marketplace.)

> Unused system function should be similarly reviewed

   Almost all modern warehouse management systems are rich enough in function that no warehouse is likely to use every feature available; in addition, some features are mutually exclusive. As time passes and as the business changes, therefore, a review of unused function can be very worthwhile. This review can turn up significant value that can be implemented at quite reasonable cost.

Unused function reviews are most often done by system suppliers, but can also be done internally or by third parties. That can either be done together with a system audit, or separately, depending on timing and need.

➤ Available system upgrades and new releases should be monitored

Warehouse management system suppliers almost always invest a portion of their profit in a program of continuing system enhancement and usually release new versions and upgrades periodically. Each release should be evaluated and, where indicated, installed. See the section below on upgrades for a more detailed discussion.

➤ Provide additional training

One is never done with system training. New workers are hired and must be given the basics. Cross-training of workers into areas they are not familiar with not only provide additional flexibility in the workforce, but also gives them insight into how the system works and allows them to make better and more effective use of it. And, from time to time, misconceptions will take root and spread through the workforce. Periodic (and brief) refresher training will pay dividends.

➤ Get involved in the user group

Most warehouse management system suppliers operate user groups, many featuring annual or semi-annual meetings and other activities. These groups are almost always well worthwhile and participation is strongly recommended. The meetings, in particular, provide a forum in which other users of the same system can be introduced to each other and can network over problems and solutions. Further, the users as a group often represent a strong "lobbying" force and may be able to exercise significant influence on the future development of the system.

Upgrades

There may or may not be clear difference between upgrades, patches and releases delivered by a warehouse management system supplier. Often, however, suppliers offer packages of new feature and function as new versions and give users the option of upgrading or remaining on their current version.

Some suppliers charge additional license fees for new versions, but others do not. License fees, however, are only a portion of the costs involved and even without them, a version upgrade is not a project to be undertaken lightly. This is especially true when custom modifications have been made to the existing version for a user.

The decision to move to up a new version of the supplier's product should be examined in detail. The study required will be significantly simpler than the initial supplier selection project, but should not be glossed over.

The decision should focus on just two alternatives: to upgrade or to stay in place. It should be based on:

> The value of the new functions and features offered by the new version. Determining this value may be simple, or may require exploration and some engineering work.

> Your need to stay current with the supplier's software. Most warehouse management system suppliers will continue to support older versions for many years, but maintaining currency enables future version upgrades and does eventually improve service from the supplier's support group

> The possibility that some custom work will no longer be needed in the upgraded system. Many warehouse management system suppliers charge separately for the support of modifications and often charge for that support at higher rates than for the base system. Eliminating custom software, therefore, has real value when it is possible.

> And, of course, the cost of doing the upgrade. This cost includes license fees, the cost of moving modifications forward when they cannot be eliminated, and cost of installation.

Maintaining Supplier Relations

Your warehouse management system represents a partnership with the supplier. By selecting and installing its software, you have effectively "married" your firm to it and, as with a human marriage, it amounts to a very long-term commitment. Therefore, it is important that you maintain a good working relationship, since divorces tend to be messy and expensive.

The warehouse management system industry has been through good times and through lean times. It now sells into a market that is near total saturation at the upper end, and is developing only slowly at the lower end. While most suppliers recognize that economic hard times can actually be good for them – because hard times drive their customers to make improvements that otherwise might be shelved – the businesses are not truly countercyclical. Rather, it seems that the industry runs on cycles of its own, possibly lagging the economy by three to five years.

Your job, of course, is to maximize value for your shareholders (or for other owners of the business) and you have additional responsibilities to your customers and employees. Maintaining a good working relationship with your warehouse management system supplier, therefore, is not one of your core responsibilities. It is, however, an important contributor to your financial results because the warehouse system itself is central to your operation. While it is possible to change warehouse management systems and suppliers, the effort is significant and the project costly. This is the primary reason for the small investment needed to periodically reach out to the supplier and to occasionally compromise when issues surface.

On the other hand, to be realistic we also need to recognize that warehouse management system suppliers vary in their attitudes and approaches to customer service. Some have been known to be simply arrogant, while others try very hard to be accommodating. You should expect excellent service, but at a price. For most warehouse management system suppliers, service is significantly more profitable than was the original installation project, so they have a great interest in keeping their existing customers.

All in all, here is a suggested program for maintaining supplier relations:

- Designate three people responsible for keeping in touch with the supplier:

    - A technical contact, who should maintain relationships with the supplier's technical force and should be in touch with them at least quarterly, even if no issues arise

    - An operations contact, which should maintain relationships with the supplier's installation project manager (or designated replacement) at least monthly. This operations contact should also be the person in your organization charged with management of your contract with the supplier and should approve supplier invoices for payment.

    - A senior management contact (possibly yourself), which should maintain contact with the supplier's senior management, exchanging phone calls at least once or twice a year.

- Develop and maintain one or more measures of the service you receive from the supplier's support organization. The measures need not be complex, but should be indicative and should be consistently measured over a long period of time. This briefing suggests:

    o   Number of incidents reported to the supplier

    o   Number of phone calls placed to a supplier as a result of an incident (excluding incidental calls to schedule, for instance, a lunch)

    o   Number of phone calls received from a supplier as a result of an incident (again excluding incidentals)

    o   Elapsed time between the reporting of an incident to receipt of the first response from the supplier

    o   Elapsed time between the reporting of an incident to receipt of final resolution

- Be an active member of your supplier's user group. Send at least one person to every user group meeting and assure that they go with an agenda, not just as casual listeners. Their agenda, for instance, might include:

    o   Making contact with as many other firms using the same system as possible. A business card collection can be valuable.

    o   Making contact with as many supplier employees as possible.

    o   Taking a written list of questions, issues and concerns, with the objective of getting answers from the supplier and parallel answers from other system users wherever possible.

    o   Creating (after the meeting is over) a brief report evaluating the experience and making recommendations for the next one.

Summary

A warehouse management system is a major investment with major but uncertain payback. As such, the project of specifying and justifying the system, selecting a supplier, and installing and operating the system is a major undertaking. History, compiled from literally thousands of firms in virtually every imaginable industry throughout the developed world, tells us that the project is well worthwhile, but also that it must be well done to produce fruit. Therefore, the best people should be used, they should receive all possible support and reasonable (if not liberal) funding, and they should be given adequate time to complete their work is a relatively unchanging environment.

The pressures of day-to-day business and the need for constant reinvention and continuous improvement in business practices and processes may make it hard to properly staff and operate a warehouse management system project to these high standards. Ultimately, all management can do is prioritize appropriately and manage to the best of its ability, but it is a good thing if the issues and concerns are acknowledged in advance.

To a degree, the warehouse management system project itself can be outsourced. Intelligent, measured and controlled outsourcing can significantly relieve your internal staff of burdens, expert knowledge can enhance project results, and the ability to concentrate on this project to the exclusion of all else can bring the project in faster. Where it makes sense, outsourcing of project work should be considered.

Appendix A – Entity Relationship Diagrams

Even for those who consider themselves non-technical, understanding the structure of a database is key to understanding the capabilities of the systems that use and maintain it. The standard entity relationship diagram is an excellent tool. With a few minutes study, much becomes clear.

Entity relationship diagrams, as their name implies, consist of two things: entities, diagrammed as boxes, and relationships, represented by lines between the boxes. The key to reading the diagrams, however, lies in understanding the line ends. Different ends define different relationships between entities.

An "entity" is typically a record on the database representing something recorded in the database. In the example to the right, there are two entities: vehicles and wheels. In this example, the two entities are related, as shown by a line. The line ends show that a vehicle can have zero or many wheels, while a wheel can be associated only with one vehicle. (Hovercraft have zero wheels, unicycles one, etc.)

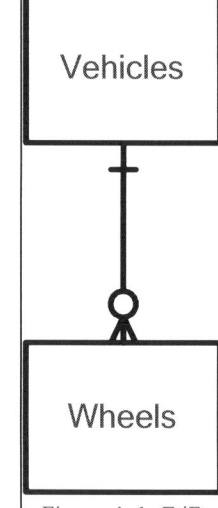

Figure A-1. E/R Diagram

When reading entity relationship diagrams, always read the line end away from the starting point. A vehicles, thus, has zero-to-many wheels, which a wheel has one and only one vehicle.

Some of the more common line ends used in entity relationship diagrams are:

Exactly one (never zero)	Either one or zero	Exactly two	Zero, one or many	One or many, but never zero	Always more than one

Appendix B – ROI Calculation Worksheet

This worksheet is intended to assist project managers and engineers in the evaluation of proposed warehouse management projects. It lists evaluations that may need to be done and quotations that may need to be obtained, provides a place to record them, and leads the user through the process of calculating the return on investment and payback period for the proposed project.

The purposes of this worksheet are (1) to remind project managers of various aspects of their projects so that cost and benefit elements are not forgotten and (2) to guide them through the calculation of ROI, Payback period, and net cost. Details of the investigation work required are left up to the user to define, but assistance in many instances is available in other white papers and worksheets.

General Instructions

1. Read through the items listed and determine which apply to your project.

2. Perform the required analyses, obtain quotations as necessary, and enter the results in the value column. Calculate totals as required

3. Calculate return on investment (ROI) and Payback per the instructions in the worksheet.

4. If ROI is either low or negative or if the payback is beyond what your business will accept, calculate net cost. In this instance, net cost is, in effect, the cost of obtaining the non-quantifiable savings and benefits.

5. If you are considering multiple suppliers or significant options, complete a separate worksheet for each.

Warehouse Management System Investment Worksheet			
Item	**Comments**	**Value**
Startup Investment[43] (SI)		
Software license fees	Include primary software and all required third-party software. Include perpetual licenses only	
Software modification	Supplier quoted price	
Computers	Hardware and operating system	
Peripherals	Printers, scanners, radio terminals, etc.	
Networks	Licensing, equipment, installation and debugging of new networks or expansion	
Network and power cabling	As required to install hardware and peripherals	
Consultation	Estimate at consultant standard rate	
In-house development	Per in-house IT quote from spec	
Facility modification	Physical change to buildings and equipment – to the extent required	
User training	As required	
Support training	For in-house support personnel	
Business downtime / disruption	Estimate value from lost business or other method	
Other	Other startup (one-time) costs	
Total Startup Investment (SI)		

---

[43] Include only future costs and not sunk costs. In other words, if you have already spent time and money evaluating a vendor, that cost is no longer relevant. If, however, you expect to spend more money on evaluation, those costs should be included. Similarly, do not include the cost of perpetual licenses you already own, equipment already in place, etc.

Ongoing Cost per Year (OC)		
Software license renewals	Unless licenses are perpetual	
Software upgrade fees	As new versions released	
Software modification upgrade fees	As required to carry modifications forward to new software versions	
Supplies	Paper, labels, forms, ink, ribbon, toner	
Energy	If significant	
Supplier license support	From all required suppliers including networks	
Supplier modification support	If supplier charges separately for support of modified software	
Hardware maintenance	Parts and labor for computer hardware and material handling equipment (if any)	
In-house support cost	Personnel and equipment – includes software and network	
Ongoing training	Includes refresher training and turnover training	
Contingencies	See page 54	
Other	Other ongoing annual costs	
Total Ongoing Cost (OC)		

Savings and Benefits per Year - Quantifiable (QSB)		
Labor cost	Include salaried and hourly personnel; prorate into full-time equivalents. Include benefits and payroll taxes as well as actual payroll cost	
Product quality	Reductions in scrap, losses, rework and returns	
Space utilization	Cost of space saved including light, heat, insurance, taxes, etc. Include leased space than can be returned to the lessor. In some instances this may better be presented as a cost avoidance.	
License non-renewals	Software license renewals no longer needed	
Support non-renewals	Support of software no longer needed. Include both in-house and supplier support	
Hardware maintenance	Parts and labor for computer hardware and material handling equipment no longer needed	
Supplies	Cost of supply items no longer needed	
Other	Other estimated savings and benefits	
Total Quantifiable Savings and Benefits QSB)		
One-Time Cost Avoidance[44] (OCA)		
Building expansion and / or construction not required due to project	Estimated cost including land acquisition, construction and one-time taxes	
Shift addition or expansion not required due to project	Cost of added supervision. Possible costs associated with reduced availability of system and equipment downtime for maintenance.	
Other	Estimated cost of other avoidances	
Total One-Time Cost Avoidance OCA)		

---

[44] Cost avoidances are future costs that will have to be spent if the proposed project is NOT done, but will not be required if the project IS done (excluding project alternatives). There can be both recurring and one-time cost avoidances.

Recurring Cost Avoidance per Year[44] (RCA)		
Building expansion and / or construction not required due to project	Taxes, maintenance and insurance on avoided construction	
Space leases not required due to project	Estimated lease costs including added taxes, utilities and insurance	
Regulatory penalties	If the project is motivated (or partly motivated) by regulatory or legal considerations, estimate the financial penalties (fines and legal costs) that it will avoid	
Labor cost	Personnel that will not have to be hired including wages, benefits, shift premiums, overtime and taxes	
Other	Estimated cost of other avoidances	
Total Recurring Cost Avoidance (RCA)		
Savings and Benefits – Non-quantifiable		
Customer service	List and describe the benefits in a separate document. Calculation of financial value not required	
Accuracy		
Product quality		
Employee convenience / satisfaction		
Management control		

Return on Investment (ROI) Calculation

To calculate return on investment, determine a project life (PL) in years[45]. Then calculate:

$$ROI = \frac{PL*(QSB + RCA - OC) - SI + OCA}{SI - OCA}$$

If ROI is negative or inadequate to fund the project, continue with the net cost calculation.

Payback Period (PP) Calculation

The project payback period (in years) is simpler than ROI:

$$PP = \frac{QSB + RCA - OC}{SI - OCA}$$

If payback is inadequate to fund the project, continue with the net cost calculation

Net Annual Cost (NAC) Calculation

To calculate net cost, calculate[46]:

$$NAC = \frac{SI - OCA}{PL} + OC - QSB - RCA$$

This figure represents the net annual cost to the business of the non-quantifiable savings and benefits. In some cases it may justify the project even in the absence of a satisfactory ROI or payback period.

---

[45] The life of a warehouse management system project is almost impossible to know in advance. Some systems have been in place and running for twenty years or more. Others are replaced almost immediately after installation. Lacking any specific knowledge, we suggest six years as an average or typical system installation life.

[46] For longer-life projects (more than three years), net annual cost should be adjusted for the time value of money. This significantly complicates the equation and, since it is unnecessary for most projects, it has not been included here.

Simply stated, money received or spent in the future is worth less than money received or spent today. To adjust, each year's net annual cost has to be calculated separately and future years have to be discounted by a "discount rate." The discounting is done by multiplying that year's net annual cost by (1-DR)^N, where DR is the discount rate and N is the number of years in the future.

Appendix C – Reference Questions

Suggested questions to ask in a reference visit (or telephone call) include:

- How long have you been using the system?

- What version of the system are you using?

- What platform does your copy run on? What DBMS do you use? What RF terminals do you use?

- How large is your warehouse? How many people work in it? How many are equipped with RF terminals?

- Why did you initially choose this supplier for your warehouse management system?

- If you had the initial system selection project to do over again, what would you do differently?

- What areas of the system did the supplier modify for you?

- Which of these modifications were done before the initial installation and which have been done subsequently?

- What modifications have been made to your system that either are now unused or have since been removed?

- Who was the supplier's project manager during your installation? What was your impression of him or her?

- Do you know (name of proposed project manager)? What is your impression of him or her?

- Did the initial installation proceed according to the supplier's schedule? If not, why not?

- Did the initially installed system meet your expectations? In what ways did it fall short?

- Have you modified the system since the initial go-live? Why? Did the modification project go well?

- ➢ Have you upgraded to a more recent version since the initial go-live? Why? Did the upgrade project go well?

- ➢ Has anyone in your company attended any of the supplier's user group meetings? What was your impression of them?

- ➢ Have you met other companies using this system? Are they satisfied with it? Can you give me names and phone numbers?

- ➢ Would you mind if we called you later in the event that additional questions come up?

It is relatively easy to add to this list in most circumstances but take care that the list does not get too long. Remember that the references you are talking to are doing you a favor.

Printed in Great Britain
by Amazon.co.uk, Ltd.,
Marston Gate.